ROY WOOD

ROY WOOD

THE MOVE, WIZZARD AND BEYOND

John Van der Kiste

With Foreword by Ray Dorset

First published by Amazon KDP 2012
Revised edition first published 2014
Printed by CreateSpace

Copyright © John Van der Kiste, 2012, 2014

Cover © Gill at Magic Arts, 2012, 2014

All rights reserved

ISBN (13-digit) 978-1502990365
ISBN (10-digit) 1502990369

CONTENTS

Foreword by Ray Dorset   3

Introduction   5

1. *Make Them Understand*   8
Early days and musical influences - the Birmingham beat boom – RW joins Mike Sheridan & the Nightriders – Formation of The Move

2. *Flowers In The Rain*   15
The Move's first gigs and increasingly controversial appearances – Tony Secunda's management – All singles from *Night Of Fear* to *Curly* – *Flowers In The Rain* controversy – 'Move' album - Ace Kefford and Trevor Burton leave – Rick Price joins – Change of management to Don Arden and then Peter Walsh, reverting to Arden - American tour – Carl Wayne leaves – 'Shazam' album

3. *Whisper In The Night*   49
RW's original concept of ELO – Jeff Lynne joins – 'Looking On' album – Rick Price leaves – *Brontosaurus* and subsequent singles up to *California Man* – Message from the Country album – Final Move appearances – First ELO album and early gigs – Growing differences between RW and Jeff Lynne, leading to RW leaving

4. *See My Baby Jive*   68
RW forms Wizzard – *Ball Park Incident* and subsequent singles to *Indiana Rainbow* – Debut gigs at Wembley and Reading – *Top Of The Pops* appearances – 'Wizzard Brew' album – Boulders album and first few solo singles – 'Introducing Eddy And The Falcons' album – US tour and meeting with Beach Boys – Cancellation of planned second US tour – Wizzard disbands

5. *Life Is Wonderful*   98

'Mustard' album – Managerial issues - Formation of Wizzo Band – BBC live gig – 'Super Active Wizzo' album and singles – Collaboration with and production for Annie Haslam on 'Annie in Wonderland' album – Wizzo Band disbands

6. *Rock City*   107

'On The Road Again' album – Production for Darts on 'Dart Attack' album – Helicopters singles and gigs – Louis Clark collaborations – 'The Singles' compilation album – Various solo singles, from *Down To Zero* onwards - The Rockers collaboration – Heartbeat 86 return to live work – 'Starting Up' album – Collaboration with Rick Wakeman

7. *Lion's Heart*   121

Sessions with Jeff Lynne – Barnardos Concert and return to regular live shows, pre-Christmas tours - Appearances at Cropredy Festival – Regular TV appearances – Millennium Night, Birmingham – Belated 'Main Street' album release – Wombles collaboration – CD reissues – Enduring popularity of *I Wish It Could Be Christmas Everyday* – Honorary Doctorate of Music at Derby University – Live tours with Status Quo – 'Music Book' compilation album

8. *…and finally*   145

Discography   147

Bibliography   162

NOTE

Throughout the book, singles, song titles, names of films, radio and TV programmes and publications are given in italics. Album titles appear in single quotation marks

FOREWORD

Firstly, I just want to say what an honour it is for me to write the foreword to a biography that is as entertaining as it is enlightening. It concerns someone I encountered several times after Mungo Jerry left the runway in 1970. One of the more memorable occasions was when he and I were on the panel of a radio quiz show transmitted from a Bristol pub. Nevertheless, as the fans might have expected, Roy was dressed in his Wizzard regalia, complete with the make-up and back-combed hair. Yet, like many so-called extroverts, he was actually quite modest, even shy about his obvious talents as a multi-instrumentalist, songwriter and record producer.

I'd first heard of him in the mid-1960s via music press coverage of The Move, a band from Birmingham, that was at the forefront of the British psychedelic scene. Every review I read was a positive one, enthusing over their dynamic stage act, enhanced as it was by their pioneering use of lighting effects and antics that involved hacking up effigies of world political figures before turning their attention to imploding televisions.

I witnessed this for myself at the Windsor Jazz and Blues Festival in August 1966 - but just as impressive was the quality of the musicianship, vocal harmonies - and the original material, all of it composed by Roy, the group's creative pivot.

It wasn't until an edition of *Top Of The Pops* in spring 1972 that I actually met him. Mungo Jerry was in the charts with *Open Up* - and The Move with *California Man*, their final hit before evolving into The Electric Light Orchestra (ELO). As an indication of how maddeningly catchy that song was - and is - shortly after that, me and the rest of Mungo Jerry were singing an *omnes fortissimo California Man* in my Mercedes on the way back from a gig at Cirencester University.

As we approached a T-junction, I decided, for a laugh, to drive us into the field opposite. Unfortunately, I didn't notice the wall and the ditch in the way. As a result, the car was wrecked, but even as we were rescued by an Irish Show Band, we were still blasting out *California Man*!

Ray Dorset aka Mungo Jerry

INTRODUCTION

In 1985, after trying to persuade one or two publishers in my idea for a book on the life and work of Roy Wood and not succeeding, I went down the self-publication route and produced *The Roy Wood Story*. It was a short fanzine-type booklet, 56 pages in length, including a 14,000-word text and eight-page discography, typeset (or, more accurately, hammered out) on a BBC Wordwise computer with dot matrix printer and published under my own imprint. Thanks mainly to a very favourable review in *Record Collector*, which appeared with remarkably good timing the following spring one month after the magazine had run my article and discography on Roy Wood and Wizzard, the response was very satisfying and my initial printing of about 100 sold out within a few weeks, necessitating a second pull.

I had been working very much in isolation, armed only with a pile of yellowing music weeklies and monthly rock magazines, a small handful of books, my record collection and the memory of one who had been devotedly following Roy's career ever since first seeing The Move playing *Night Of Fear* on *Top Of The Pops* in 1967. Within a few months my knowledge had been supplemented considerably by other fans more than keen to pool their resources by sending me photocopies, cuttings and cassettes of material I had missed and never known about. Coincidentally *Face The Music*, a fanzine devoted to ELO, Roy Wood, The Move, and all closely-associated acts, to which I was happy to become a regular contributor, was about to be launched and went from strength to strength over its ten years and twenty-four issues before making the transition from print to an online service. Meanwhile I was regularly asked if I planned to update my project. Lack of time and work on other books delayed this for over twenty years, and neither I nor my readership ever thought it would happen.

Better late than never. When I finally came round to producing this successor to it a quarter of a century later, the world around us had changed in many ways. Microsoft Word was now state-of-the art, self-publishing had moved into print on demand and the electronic age, while e-mail and the internet made it easy to check on facts which would have previously taken a letter or phone call that might never be answered or returned. YouTube had made it possible for us to watch old clips from *Top Of The Pops, The Old Grey Whistle Test* and other TV shows that we thought we would never see again (or missed first time round), live gigs, interviews, and even hear material that had never been released on record, more often than not thanks to major labels no longer keen to issue new product by anybody over the age of 35.

Even more importantly, vinyl had become virtually a museum piece, non-charting albums which had been deleted within weeks of release because of poor sales and could generally only be obtained through persistent hunting at major secondhand record dealers or record fairs, sometimes at exorbitant sums, were remastered and reissued at competitive prices on CD, generally supplemented with out-takes and previously unreleased material, and very elusive singles which fetched the equivalent of a king's ransom could likewise be found on CD compilations and were now readily available at the click of a mouse. As for the five-inch silver laser disc, this was starting to give way to the ubiquitous MP3 download and Spotify. The original black vinyl pressings could often be located online, though regrettably at the cost of putting many a well-established record shop or high street chain out of business, or alternatively compelling them to transfer their business to the internet.

Some of the 7" singles remain far from cheap. *Dance Around The Maypole* by Acid Gallery, the sole legitimate release of which on CD appears to have been on the 4-CD 'Nuggets II: Original Artyfacts From the British Empire And Beyond' longform box compilation released in 2001 but long since deleted, is valued in mint condition by the most recent annual edition of *Record Collector Rare Price Guide* at £55, and *Rock'n'Roll Christian* by Grunt Futtock, which has yet to be issued on the new digital medium, at £30. For their relevance and Roy Wood connections, you will need to read the rest of the book. 'Nuggets II' itself would have set you back at least £65 on Amazon Marketplace the last time I checked. Finally, *I Wish It Could be Christmas Everyday* had become an evergreen fixture not only at Christmas parties and on radio playlists or TV light entertainment shows every December, but also a recurrent re-entry in the British charts, even though the days of purchasing it brand new on seven inches of black vinyl over the counter may now be almost as distant a memory as the ten-inch shellac discs it had replaced.

This is a totally unauthorised work, written by an enthusiastic but objective fan. I owe a considerable debt to the pioneering interviews of others from various press and internet sources, as well as to friends happy to share anecdotes and knowledge. It has also been my pleasure to have met and spoken briefly at various times to Roy Wood, Bev Bevan (and obtain their autographs – thanks guys) and the late Carl Wayne. I was also honoured and delighted to be given the opportunity to write the booklet notes to some of the various Move, Wizzard and Roy Wood CD releases that have appeared on EMI and Music Club over the last couple of decades.

In updating and expanding the work, firstly as an e-book only and two years later as a paperback, my particular thanks go to Ray Dorset for his excellent Foreword; Alan Clayson, Paul Cox, Neil Hardie, Lynn Hoskins, Steve May, Paul Ogden, and Miles Tredinnick for their help and the benefit of their knowledge in various ways, especially reminiscences and the provision of extensive lists and cuttings; to Rob Griffiths, Colin Webb, Fraser Massey, Dave and Sue Morgan, and *Record Collector*, for the publicity they gave me with the first edition; to Mark Paytress, whose notes on the Move reissued and remastered CDs on Salvo are exemplary and a mine of information, to my old mate and erstwhile collaborator Derek Wadeson who conducted an interview - with some input from me - with Roy in *Keep On Rockin*, the 1970s fanzine we jointly founded, edited and wrote for fourteen issues between 1991 and 1996, and above all and finally indefatigable fans and project managers Gill at Magic Arts (cheers for the cover), Martin Kinch and Rob Caiger, all of whom have between them been regular sources of info and contributed in major ways towards making this book possible, and to my wife Kim for her help and support throughout.

John Van der Kiste, 2012, 2014

1. *MAKE THEM UNDERSTAND*

1946 was the first full year of peace after the privations and horrors of World War Two for a proud and victorious but weary Great Britain. Gramophone records still played at 78 rpm, and the pop singles of the day were 10" in diameter. The 12" 33 rpm long-player and the 7" 45 rpm single would begin to transform the listening habits of the public before the decade was out, although the first weekly singles chart, a Top 12 (or rather Top 15, as some records tied for the twelve positions) was still six years away.

It was also a particularly good year in terms of the arrival of several individuals in Britain whose talents would help to shape the development of popular music some two or three decades hence. Syd Barrett was born in January, exactly two months before fellow Pink Floyd member David Gilmour, while March would also be the month that Tony Ashton, Ray Dorset of Mungo Jerry and Andy Bown of The Herd and subsequently Status Quo, entered the world. In April it was the turn of Slade guitarist Dave Hill, and Mud vocalist Les Gray, in May of Donovan Leitch, Dave Mason of Traffic, Robert Fripp of King Crimson, and Mick Ronson, guitarist with David Bowie, Ian Hunter and others; in June of Noddy Holder, John Lawton of Uriah Heep, and Ian McDonald of King Crimson and later Foreigner; in July of Andy Mackay of Roxy Music, and Bon Scott of AC/DC; in August of Keith Moon; in September of Barry Gibb, Freddie Mercury, and drummers Don Powell of Slade, plus John Coghlan of Status Quo; and in October of Peter Green, and Dan McCafferty of Nazareth.

The following month, on 8 November, Roy Wood was born at Eddish Road, Yardley, Birmingham. For a long time the legend persisted that he had been given the forenames Ulysses Adrian, as many a work of rock reference would state in print. Only some forty years later was it confirmed to the world at large that this was nothing more, nothing less than a time-honoured joke. Thanks to somebody in The Move's entourage around the start of their career who filled in a 'lifelines' form for the press, giving (or purporting to give) personal information about each member, and bestowing these fictitious names on him for a laugh, it stuck until a little investigation and examination of the birth certificate proved that the post-war baby was born and registered simply as Roy Wood.

This new arrival was part of a musical family with a brother and two sisters all much older than him, one of whom sang with a big band shortly after the war. With music all around him, it must have seemed that his vocation in life would be obvious from the start. 'When I was really small,' he recalled, 'my Mum and Dad were classical music fans, and we had an old radiogram, and used to play all kinds of stuff. I think their favourite two composers were Rossini and Tchaikovsky at that time – that's why I grew up to be a bit of a Tchaikovsky fan, because he really wrote some nice tunes, as did Elgar, who became my favourite after that.'

A brother-in-law was a big band jazz fan, 'and through that, this is the only music tuition I ever had in my life – on drums when I was five. I played drums with a big band when I was six at my sister's wedding, and I was absolutely chuffed about it, because the guy who taught me was in the band and let me have a go.' Soon he was also playing harmonica in working men's clubs.

Another of the defining moments for him came at the end of the 1950s. 'When I was twelve years old I saw The Shadows playing at Birmingham Town Hall, and that was it for me. Hank Marvin's guitar sounded like it had been dipped in dettol or something like that – it was the cleanest sound in the world. I just couldn't forget it, and I nagged my Dad for ever after that until he bought me a guitar.'

The rock'n'roll flame was kept alive, when as a teenager he was thrilled to see Little Richard and Gene Vincent performing onstage at various times. Coincidentally Vincent was managed by Don Arden, who would later appear somewhat prominently in Roy's professional career. He would have been too young to see Eddie Cochran, who died in 1960 from injuries received in a road accident while on tour in Britain. But as 'the first person to play all his own instruments on his records' as well as the writer and singer of so many rock'n'roll classics, Eddie was also an abiding influence on the budding teenage Birmingham guitarist.

By the time he reached his teens he was beginning to teach himself every musical instrument he could get his hands on, an accurate forecast of the shape of things to come for a man who would seem equally at ease with almost any of them. He would disappear for school, wait for his parents to leave the house, and then nip back smartly to spend the day practising. Leaving Moseley School of Art at the age of 16 - not actually expelled, but given permission to leave early, as he later put it - he worked successively as a signwriter, a welder, and a greengrocer. But all of these took a poor second place to his guitar.

According to a much-quoted poem by Philip Larkin, 'So life was never better than in nineteen sixty-three'. It was certainly a vintage year for the British beat boom. In Liverpool the Beatles, the Searchers, and Gerry and the Pacemakers between them all ensured a virtual Merseybeat stranglehold at the top of the singles chart for much of the year. Down south in Dagenham, Brian Poole and the Tremeloes, who had narrowly beaten the Beatles to a contract with Decca Records at the start of the previous year, partly as they were based nearer London and partly as they presented a more professional appearance, were likewise enjoying one hit single after another. On the western fringes of the capital, the less clean-cut, more rebellious Rolling Stones had just started building themselves a sizeable following for their earthy brand of rhythm'n'blues, while trad jazz was being elbowed out by the blues boom which was represented by the likes of its godfathers Alexis Korner and John Mayall alongside their protégés Eric Clapton, Jimmy Page, the Mann-Hugg Blues Brothers, shortly to become Manfred Mann, and a little later Peter Green's Fleetwood Mac. Some of these musicians wisely kept one foot in the more commercial, more lucrative pop industry, and Page's session work as a guitarist could be heard on many a hit single by other artists, from The Who and The Kinks to Petula Clark and Herman's Hermits.

Meanwhile, in Birmingham there was a clutch of lesser-known but no less active groups. Among them were Ronnie and the Renegades, Johnny Neal and the Starliners, Denny Laine and the Diplomats, Pat Wayne and the Beachcombers, Danny King and the Mayfair Set, and the Rockin' Berries – the only one from this list to chalk up any major hits – to name but a few. The top Brum groups could average six or more local gigs a week in city clubs, with each member taking home around £30. Their repertoire came from the standard chart fare, including every Beatles single as it came out, Cliff Richard and the Shadows hits, and later a sprinkling of Motown and soul covers. The first Brum beat record was *Sugar Baby* by Jimmy Powell and the Dimensions, issued in March 1962, while the first which would sell enough to make the national top ten was the Applejacks' *Tell Me When* two years later.

After a brief stint with the Falcons, whose name would be resurrected briefly for an album by Wizzard some twelve years later, Roy turned professional with Gerry Levene and the Avengers, who also included Mike Hopkins on guitar, Jim Onslow on bass, and future Moody Blues drummer Graeme Edge.

Looking back many years later, Onslow recalled that Roy was 'very shy but still had that little bit of a crazy spark but seemed to be looking for something, I don't think he knew what, but he kept looking and eventually found it.'. With them he recorded one single on Decca, *Dr Feelgood*, released in January 1964. All the local bands changed their personnel regularly, and it was not long before Roy moved on. As one of two lead guitarists, he felt they lacked something and he had more to offer. The group folded shortly after his departure, with Graeme Edge becoming a founder member of the Moody Blues alongside Denny Laine and ex-Falcon John Lodge.

Around this time Norrie Paramor, who had produced several hits for Cliff Richard and The Shadows, came on a talent-spotting mission to Birmingham with the aim of re-creating a new Liverpool-style boom in the Midlands city. A massive two-day audition of hopeful combos was held at the Moathouse Club, and Mike Sheridan and the Nightriders passed with flying colours. They went on to record two singles for Columbia which fell just short of the Top 50, before guitarist 'Big Al' Johnson left. Prior to his departure, he sat in on the audition to choose his successor.

Of all the dozen-odd optimists who turned up in the queue to join the one local band which really seemed to be working and pulling the money in, clutching their guitars and amps, Roy was the winner. Mike initially had his misgivings about this rather unusual-looking character with long black dyed hair plastered to his face and big pointy toed shoes, dressed in a mixture of clothing made by his sister plus odds and sods from the Oxfam shop, who did not look exactly right for a well-groomed cabaret group. But he knew his

Chuck Berry licks, learnt the set very quickly and threw in a few ideas of his own, could hit the high notes with ease, and could also teach them vocal harmonies.

With regard to the others there was no contest, and he was in the group in time to play on their third single, *What A Sweet Thing That Was*. These were the days when both sides of a single were recorded in a three-hour session if the band were lucky, and any bum notes stayed there as time and finance did not allow any other way. Though the new record fared no better than the first two, Mike readily acknowledged that Roy had changed the group for the better. Before his arrival they had been 'very straight', but he was such an offbeat character that he soon altered all that. When not getting them into vocal harmonies, he helped to expand their repertoire, and showed them there were more than three chords. Already he was acquiring a local reputation as no mean guitarist, and at around the same time he played on a single by Danny King's Mayfair Set, *Pretty Things,* released in January 1965, the same month as the Nightriders' fourth, *Here I Stand*.

Later that year they changed their name to Mike Sheridan's Lot, and put out two more singles with the same line-up. The first, *Take My Hand*, in August 1965, featured Roy's debut as a songwriter on the B-side, *Make Them Understand*. As Mike later recalled, it was influenced by the style of Tom Jones' *It's Not Unusual*, but 'it came out very bad for us. The song was all right, it was just the way we did it.' Some years later Mike signed the sleeve of a copy belonging to a fan with the words, 'Roy Wood's first song and he's got me to thank for wrecking it!!!' Roy would later admit himself that it was not very good - but then everybody has to start somewhere.

It was one of a large batch he had written, but the rest were shelved as cover versions always went down better on stage. Roy's first compositions had been instrumentals, inspired by his having seen and heard the Shadows. It was only after the advent of the Beatles, whose original compositions blazed the trail for everyone else, that he started writing proper songs. But from earlier days he had always had a way with words, having written a book of fairy stories for adults 'with weird twists at the end' during his art college days.

By now they were appearing regularly on ATV's *Five O'Clock Club*. Locally they had made a name for themselves partly on account of Roy's guitar work, and partly for their comedy stage routine. The Rockin' Berries had started introducing comedy routines into their act, and Mike thought they should likewise try their hand as they had the potential to do it, so they put together a short routine based around 'the Jimmy Savile show'. Roger Spencer did an impersonation of the then renowned but later posthumously-disgraced BBC presenter, while Mike did P.J. Proby, and Roy would impersonate Donovan and Dusty Springfield, the latter complete with white wig and pink bow. This was all done, he stressed later, 'in an extremely masculine manner.' Such mimicry was an accurate forecast of what was eventually to come on his records.

One more flop single, *Don't Turn Your Back On Me, Babe* in December 1965, marked the beginning of the end. The song was a Jackie de Shannon composition, produced for them by Norman Smith, who went on to produce Pink Floyd, and to have hits as a solo performer in the early 1970s himself as Hurricane Smith. All of the group were disillusioned by their continual lack of chart success, and at length Roy announced that he was leaving. The Nightriders continued with a new guitarist, but Roy proved a hard act to follow. Mike Sheridan left a while later, and he was replaced with another young ambitious Brummie, Jeff Lynne. Soon afterwards they changed their name to the Idle Race.

Roy had been jamming on a regular basis with other musicians at the Cedar Club in Birmingham, a venue where all the local bands used to play. Any musicians who had a night off between gigs would generally gather there anyway just to see which band was playing, and maybe pick up a few ideas from them. Among them were members of Carl Wayne and the Vikings, another act who had long been frustrated by doing the same round of city clubs with their repertoire of half-hearted crowd-pleasing cover versions. They had however released a couple of singles on Pye, *What's A Matter Baby* and *This Is Love,* plus a third, *My Girl*, issued on ABC in the US only. Their line-up included Chris (Ace) Kefford on bass and latterly Bev Bevan on drums.

Playing other people's songs, mostly current chart material, proved rather stifling for most of the musicians after a while, and some of them longed to do their own. At the bar one night, some of them discussed how fed up they were with being little more than a human jukebox. Roy mentioned that he had a few songs of his own that he would like to try out, and several said they were interested in hearing them. At around the same time, Ace Kefford and guitarist Trevor Burton from Danny King's Mayfair Set were in the audience one night to see Davy Jones and the Lower Third. Talking afterwards to Davy, who was shortly to achieve worldwide fame under the name of David Bowie, the suggestion was made to them that they should form a band themselves.

Danny was asked to join them as vocalist, but he turned the offer down. They then spoke to Carl Wayne (real name Colin David Tooley), who was not only a versatile singer and accomplished front man, but also slightly older and more experienced, and had a good reputation for being able to get his band work. More importantly, he was prepared to leave the Vikings if there was the chance of joining a band who were prepared to set their sights a little higher. Rumour had it that at one stage he was also sought as a vocalist by the Spectres, a London-based outfit who had recorded for Pye's Piccadilly label, and would achieve immortality when they decided a couple of years later to call themselves The Status Quo (soon to drop the 'The' in their name).

As drummer their first choice was John Bonham, who was then playing in the Way Of Life with Ace's uncles and would later be part of Led Zeppelin, but there were personal issues between him and Carl and he turned the offer down. Next they approached Bev Bevan, who was happy to join. With Roy on lead guitar and backing vocals, the combination seemed right.

Thus The Move was born, a name thought up by Roy as each member had played in other bands and it was 'a big sort of move thing'. In addition, like The Who, it was a short sharp simple name which would look good on advertising. This new, eager-to-go line-up gave them perhaps their last chance of breaking out of the Brum circuit and making a national name for themselves. The Moody Blues had shown it could be done, and had raised the bar by starting off the year 1965 with a No. 1 single in *Go Now*.

The Move would not be far behind in likewise making a name for themselves.

2. *FLOWERS IN THE RAIN*

The Move played their first gig at the Belfry Hotel in Sutton Coldfield on 18 January 1966. One of their contemporaries who had no doubt in their ability to find success on a wider scale was an old friend of Bev's, Bobby Davis, later to find fame as comedian Jasper Carrott. He had slammed Bev's previous groups as a load of rubbish. After hearing The Move in action, he agreed they were by far the best of the lot. Likewise Mike Sheridan had previously told Roy he was wasting his time. The Move, he said, was a stupid name, and when he heard his guitarist was joining this new band and had also been invited to join the already established Tony Rivers and the Castaways, he told Roy that Rivers was a more likely bet. But Roy chose to disregard the advice and stick with his instincts. Mike came to see their initial gig, and admitted that despite his initial reservations they really were brilliant.

The Move's initial repertoire mixed American rock and soul covers, particularly Impressions, Four Tops songs and Motown in general, though in a more rock kind of way, and with four- and five-part harmonies. Few if any other bands of that size could boast a group where every member was capable of taking a turn at the mike for a lead vocal. (The Beatles could, admittedly – but there were only four of them.) Many of their ideas as to which songs they should feature in their act came from Danny King, who was reputed to have the best record collection in Birmingham.

But they always had ambitions to be far more than just another covers band. Roy had already penned a B-side, and with several more songs up his sleeve, he was the obvious writer with a talent to be developed. He also had a clear idea of the sound they were aiming for – 'as powerful as the Who, and vocally like the Beach Boys'. The Pretty Things, who also had a reputation for being pretty wild onstage, were likewise sometimes cited as an influence.

January 1966 was also the month that the band entered a recording studio for the first time, at Johnny Haines' Ladbrooke Sound Recording in Birmingham. Among the songs they laid down were four written by Roy, *You're The One I Need*, with Ace on lead vocal, and Roy, Carl and Trevor taking turns respectively on *Winter Song, I Know Your Face,* and *The Fugitive*. Several numbers from their live set were also included, among them *I Can't Hear You No More*, previously recorded by Betty Everett, Brenda Lee's *Is It True*, the Isley Brothers' *Respectable*, the Orlons' *Don't Hang Up*, and the Marvelettes' *Too Many Fish In The Sea*. *You're The One I Need* and three of the covers were broadcast as a session on local radio the following month, and eventually found release as the opening tracks on The Move's 'Anthology' in 2008.

But Roy's songwriting talents were not the only vital ingredient in getting them known nationally. Much of that was down to Tony Secunda, who had already managed the Moody Blues. The promoter at the Belfry knew him, rang him up and asked him if he would come and see The Move on stage. Secunda saw himself as one of the new streetwise group managers following in the traditions of Andrew Loog Oldham, the Rolling Stones' Svengali, and Kit Lambert and Chris Stamp, who had done likewise for The Who. He came up to the Belfry and the Cedar Club, was immediately convinced of their potential, signed them up to his management, and allocated them a dedicated personal photographer, Bobby Davidson.

In landing them a support slot at the London Marquee, Wardour Street, on 1 April, which became a regular headline gig on Thursdays from June, he left nothing to chance. What counted in his terms was not just music – it was image as well. What would make them stand out from all the rest, and get them noticed? They had a choice of being either a clean-cut wholesome pop group, the kind that mums and dads could like as well as the kids, or else something more anarchic like the Rolling Stones. It was a lesson was obviously not lost on Malcolm McLaren in his promotion of the Sex Pistols a decade later.

Dressed as Chicago gangsters, The Move quickly acquired a reputation as wild men on stage, the sort of which no parent would approve. Busts of Adolf Hitler and rebel Rhodesian leader Ian Smith were reduced to pieces as a matter of routine. En route to a gig, the band would stop off to buy one or two cheap secondhand TV sets, take them on stage, and hack them to pieces as the climax to their act, allegedly as a gesture against the one-eyed monster which had people glued passively to their chairs for hour after hour. Cadillacs soon assumed the same role, with cars being chopped up by the lads to show that they were only lumps of scrap metal if hammered hard enough. Such behaviour must have been a distressing incitement to frustrated motor owners up and down the country. Even if the hapless vehicle was accompanied on stage by a pair of strippers, the audience generally seemed less fascinated by the sight of feminine flesh than mechanical violence.

On one occasion, Carl Wayne got carried away and reduced the main part of Stourbridge Town Hall stage to firewood. Another time, Roy lost part of the side of his shoe after Carl got a little carried away (to paraphrase the title of an early Pink Floyd track, 'Careful with that axe, Carl'), but thankfully his foot remained intact. Those in authority hated The Move, but Fleet Street loved them as they could often be relied on to provide good copy.

While the group were happy, or at least prepared, to go along with this role to a certain extent, it was not really them. But as Carl said, Secunda was determined that they were 'going to be a hard band, not a namby-pamby band, and it really wasn't in our nature.' Roy, he insisted, was 'a gentle person at heart, a really sweet fella, and for him to be stuck with The Move's image was farcical.'

A few months into their residency, they proved too hot for the Marquee to handle. One night in November, their roadie Allen Harris decided that the crowd might be rather bored with the TV-smashing routine by now. Feeling that something more dramatic was called for, he let off a load of smoke bombs, leaving Secunda to go to the nearest telephone box and call the police and fire brigade. An angry John Gee, the Marquee manager, told reporters that the group had gone too far this time. He omitted to mention that when he tried to stop Carl from setting light to the stage, the latter tore Gee's wig off and threw it into the flames. That was the end of their residency at the Marquee.

All these acts of destruction were the brainchild of Secunda and to some extent photographer Davidson. For a while the band were caught up in the sheer excitement of it and nobody entered into the spirit of it with more enthusiasm than Carl Wayne, the lead vocalist and the only one not encumbered by a guitar or a drum kit. Yet looking back on it some years later, the vocalist would say that he was amazed they managed to get away with it – and not cause more serious damage than they did.

The stunts had not been limited to their live act. When a general election was called for March 1966 by Labour Prime Minister Harold Wilson, anxious to go to the country for the comfortable working majority that his wafer-thin victory in October 1964 had failed to give him, The Move found another opportunity to grab a news story or two. During the campaign, they posed cheerfully for the papers alongside a MOVE WITH THE TORIES – VOTE CONSERVATIVE poster. They also invited the Conservative leader Edward Heath, who was well known for his love of music as a hobby, to play organ at a gig in aid of party funds. Owing to his 'extremely busy programme', the Leader of Her Majesty's Opposition was unable to accept their 'kind invitation'. Perhaps there was some irony in the fact that in 1966 the minimum voting age was still 21, which meant that only two of them, Carl and Bev, were as yet qualified to cast their vote at elections.

One bid for a story in the tabloid press, not the most successful, involved their walking around Manchester and holding up traffic as they carried a cardboard hydrogen bomb around the streets for a couple of hours. Secunda played a skilful double game, hiding in the crowd, shouting out how disgraceful it was and calling for someone to arrest the individuals responsible. Perhaps unfortunately for them nobody took much notice, the police refused to play along with it and merely told them to move on. (They must have seen it all several times before). A photographer took a picture of them as Secunda, somehow managing to keep a straight face, pleaded with reporters that he did not want any cheap publicity. The papers said that The Move had been arrested while making an anti-Vietnam protest, but it was hardly the notorious gesture they had been trying to make.

But they also had positive reviews for their live work, and not just for the more notorious showmanship or innovative features such as their being the first group in Britain to use front projection of colour film as part of the performance. On 30 July 1966, after watching England's victory in the World Cup final on TV at Secunda's London apartment, they went to play at the three-day sixth National Jazz and Blues Festival at Windsor Racecourse. In a bill headlined by Cream, and also featuring the Spencer Davis Group and the Small Faces among others, they stole the show, even earning praise from columnists on the quality papers.

When they had built up sufficient experience and repertoire, it was time to look for a record label. Producer Joe Boyd tried to convince Jac Holzman to sign them to Elektra, but without success. Another producer, Denny Cordell, had known Secunda since they had worked together with the Moody Blues. Cordell was forming the New Breed production company with music publisher David Platz and they signed The Move, initially leasing the recordings to Decca's new experimental label Deram Records. Even then, the process made news as the contract was signed on the back of a topless model, Liz Wilson. How long before she was allowed to wash it off is not recorded, but this was one contract which could hardly be stored for posterity in a filing cabinet.

1966 had marked a turning point in rock music. The three biggest names of that age had all issued seminal LPs during the summer - the Beatles, 'Revolver', the Rolling Stones, 'Aftermath', and Bob Dylan, rock's first double LP, 'Blonde On Blonde'. Between them, these platters showed that contemporary music need no longer be restricted to the conventional, vocal-guitar-bass-drums, three-minute song format, easily reproduced on stage. Songs or jams which burst the three-minute barrier wide open, and the use of phasing, reversed tape, or whatever else producer and engineer could concoct, all had their part. The use of additional instruments showed that there was more to pop instrumentation than the normal guitars, drums, keyboards and occasional strings or brass arrangements, particularly on 'Aftermath', on which the ever-versatile Brian Jones played sitar, marimbas, harpsichord and dulcimer as well as lead and rhythm guitars. At the same time, the Beach Boys' painstakingly-constructed *Good Vibrations* and the Four Tops' ambitiously-arranged *Reach Out I'll Be There* proved that there was room at the top of the British singles chart for 45s which dared to take the three-minute pop song into more ambitious territory. Finally, anticipating the days when albums would become more important than singles, by the end of the year Pink Floyd, Cream and the Jimi Hendrix Experience were about to come very respectable names to drop.

The first Move product, which was recorded at Advision Studios, London, in October 1966 and released in December, contained two Roy Wood compositions (as did the next four singles), *Night of Fear*, and *Disturbance*. The group had wanted to make the eerie *Disturbance* complete with mock Hammer horror screams from Cordell and Secunda at the end, the A-side, but the record company felt it was the less commercial of the two.

Within less than two and a half minutes, *Night Of Fear* incorporated a menacingly heavy guitar riff taken unashamedly from the final movement of Tchaikovsky's *1812 Overture*, and lyrics which were immediately interpreted as being about a bad trip, with shared vocal lines and harmonies that sounded pretty and pretty fierce all at once. Keen to court controversy, Secunda stated that the song was about someone who had had a nightmare after taking a stale dose of LSD. Roy, who had written the song (on banjo, of all instruments), said it was merely about hearing noises in the night and not being able to sleep. Bev backed up the drug-free innocence of his friend's lyrics, explaining that Roy had always been a prolific writer of stories while he was at school, and several of them would provide the inspiration for what could be taken as some of the group's more chemically-induced music. It entered the charts at the start of the new year and in its fourth week reached No. 2, only held off the top spot by the Monkees' *I'm a Believer*. Modestly, Roy later said he 'didn't think it was good enough,' but when it succeeded, it gave him the incentive to continue writing.

To a casual observer the follow-up, *I Can Hear The Grass Grow*, sounded as though it could have been equally drug-inspired. In fact, the title had been suggested by Davidson, who had been in the offices of the naturist magazine *Health & Efficiency* and had overheard a remark about the letter from a reader who said she enjoyed listening to pop music because 'where I live it's so bloody quiet that I can hear the grass grow'. What a great title for a song that would make, he told Roy, who lost no time in getting some ideas together and completing one. Released in March 1967 and reaching No. 5, it was subsequently covered as a single by American band the Blues Magoos, while in their early days Sweet recorded their version for the occasional Radio 1 session, and in 1996 Status Quo did likewise on their first album of cover versions, 'Don't Stop'. It was later hailed as a classic British Freakbeat record, although the term was not coined until about twenty years later. Most famously, perhaps, a copy was also one of the 7" singles that long-serving radio DJ and indefatigable record collector John Peel kept in a battered wooden box at his home, containing a selection which had always meant a good deal to him. The B-side, *Wave The*

Flag And Stop The Train, was an attempt to emulate the Monkees' style.

Grass, of course, was not just an innocent type of vegetation which grew on lawns and in fields. The band members' attitude to drugs was widely divergent. Roy and Bev, who never smoked, did not even touch the stuff, even though the press were all too ready to suggest that the first two hits had been written about chemically-induced trips. When Carl, who was happy enough with a pint and a cigarette, was offered a joint at a party in London he declined, saying he had just eaten. Later he took a tab of acid, and hated every minute of the experience, vowing there would not be a second time. On the other hand Trevor and Ace were more than happy to indulge. Trevor came through it, he would recall, without any of the negative experiences, but Ace admitted that it 'did his head in'.

Despite their new-found fame, The Move stayed close to their roots, and still lived in Birmingham. For them, there would be none of this superstar nonsense of buying luxury mansions in the stockbroker belt, although like many other showbiz names, Carl would later find it made sense for business reasons to make his home in London.

Nothing succeeds like excess, they say. Secunda believed it, though even he may have had mixed feelings about his protégés' bad boy image when they were excluded from the bill on the Walker Brothers' package tour in April by the Top Rank Organisation, who declared they were 'not suitable'. Ironically they chose the Jimi Hendrix Experience, hardly a family-friendly cabaret act themselves, to fill the vacant slot.

The Move did however appear at the fourteen-hour Technicolor Dream at Alexandra Palace, north London, on 29 April. A fund-raising gig for the *International Times*, and the first event of its kind in Britain to attract more than 10,000 people, it had a line-up which also included Alexis Korner, Graham Bond, the Pretty Things, Pink Floyd, Tomorrow, the Soft Machine, John's Children with the still virtually unknown Marc Bolan on vocals, and the Crazy World of Arthur Brown. Although neither he nor the rest of the Rolling Stones were playing on the bill, Brian Jones was among those present, and approved of The Move's stage act. 'They really are an extension of the Stones' idea of smashing conventions,' he told music journalist Keith Altham. 'Destroying TV sets, etc is all part of dissatisfaction with convention.' More praise came from another illustrious member of the audience. As Roy was walking towards the stage from the dressing room, John Lennon in his Afghan coat passed him, did a soldier-like halt in front of him and saluted. Roy saluted him back, and as he walked on he heard Lennon say to the person he was with, 'He's brilliant.'

The event was a curtain raiser to what would always be remembered as the summer of love, the flower power era, with Scott McKenzie, Eric Burdon and the Animals, and the Flowerpot Men among those exhorting all and sundry to come to San Francisco, not forgetting to wear some flowers in their hair. The Beatles' 'Sergeant Pepper's Lonely Hearts Club Band' had revolutionised everyone's perception of what LPs should be like, having tapped - or prevailed on producer George Martin to tap - new horizons in sound and studio technology. ('Sergeant Pepper' would however soon become the despair of other producers, having made self-indulgence and a costly six-month timetable for recording LPs respectable among lesser groups). The imprisonment of Mick Jagger and Keith Richard on charges of possessing drugs in June, albeit for only one night before being granted bail and released, brought forth a signed editorial from William Rees-Mogg in *The Times*, headed 'Who breaks a butterfly on a wheel?' (a quote from eighteenth-century poet Alexander Pope), protesting at the severity of their sentences, which were soon quashed.

On 22 July The Move played a 'Free the Pirates' benefit gig at Alexandra Palace, sponsored by Radio Caroline, in protest at the government's attempts to silence and criminalise the pirate radio stations with the Wireless Telegraphy Act, later the Marine Broadcasting (Offences) Act. Appropriately the climax of the act was when Carl took an axe to a full-size effigy of Harold Wilson. Nonetheless the Act became law three weeks later.

As aware as anyone that psychedelia was a fad with no future, Carl told reporters that The Move were not psychedelic, 'we're showmen'. Nevertheless the group were content to play along with the image. It was amply demonstrated by single number three, a song that captured the essence of the time perfectly, *Flowers In The Rain*. Even so, in its recorded form it owed much to The Move's co-producer and arranger, New Yorker Tony Visconti, who had come to London as Denny Cordell's assistant. After the initial recording,

Cordell was unhappy with the performance and production, and wanted to drop it.

Visconti, who loved the song, had more faith. 'It was during that period when every time the Beatles brought out a new single, you'd hear some new instrument on it like a sitar, a cello or a French horn, or something like that,' he said later. He begged to be allowed to experiment with putting some woodwind on it, and scored parts for oboe, flute, clarinet and French horn, as a complement to the pastoral flavour of the song's lyrics. The four classical musicians were hired for the job at a cost of £12 each. With his knowledge of the classics, Visconti paid homage to Mendelssohn's *Spring Song* which he quoted in the outro. The quartet were recorded at half speed during the song's bridge, allegedly in order to create the effect of the instruments being played by pixies sitting on mushrooms in an enchanted forest.

Similar experiments were used for the B-side, another whimsical Roy song, *(Here We Go Round The) Lemon Tree*. The band and Cordell were delighted with his work. Both tracks were recorded in July, and *Lemon Tree* was initially chosen as the A-side. At the end of the month, just as initial copies were about to be pressed, Secunda and the band decided to reverse the coupling.

This was the first record to be released on the newly-reactivated Regal Zonophone label. Originally formed in 1932, it had been one of the most popular imprints for popular music during the war years in the days of 78 rpm 10" discs, then for a while it became mainly the preserve of Salvation Army recordings. After being rested for a while it was revived by EMI to handle the Essex Music and Straight Ahead companies, and it was now about to give an outlet to The Move and Procol Harum. The latter's seminal *A Whiter Shade of Pale*, which held the No. 1 spot for six weeks that summer and was regarded as the godfather of British progressive rock, had also appeared on Deram, and the label would shortly provide a haven for Tyrannosaurus Rex and Joe Cocker. Released in August, *Flowers In The Rain* peaked at No. 2 in the charts, only held off by the year's most bankable singer, balladeer Engelbert Humperdinck, with *The Last Waltz*.

The immortality of *Flowers In The Rain* in the history of broadcasting was assured by its being the first record played in its entirety on Wonderful Radio One when Tony Blackburn opened up the BBC's new radio station, the government-approved successor to pirate broadcasting, on the morning of 30 September 1967. Maybe the irony was lost on the Corporation that the band had been playing the Free the Pirates gig only two months earlier, and that Radio 1 was the government-approved successor to the pirate stations. Moreover, Tony Blackburn was one of several former pirate radio DJs who had literally jumped ship just in time to find more secure jobs by broadcasting on the right side of the establishment tracks. Some years later, at a function attended by both, he told Roy that it had been a bit of a mad panic at Radio 1 just before they went on air. He did not know whether the records had been sorted for the show or placed in the right order, so as he was about to go on air he just dived for the first one he could lay his hands on. By pure chance, *Flowers In The Rain* happened to be the one. However, later still, Tony remarked on air while presenting *Pick of the Pops* on Radio 2 that his choice of the record was deliberate. It was a good record to launch the station, 'because of that crashing noise at the beginning'.

Unhappily Secunda was not content to stop at getting his protégés to exchange their gangster pinstripes for beads and kaftans when the photographer was around. He overstepped the mark, and cost the group dearly – Roy, as songwriter, most dearly of all - with a major *faux pas*. A friend of his had a postcard designed by cartoonist Neil Smith, libelling Harold Wilson and his secretary, Marcia Falkender, showing them in 'an objectionable pose'. Carl was the first band member to see it, and he showed it to a lawyer who advised him to keep well away from anything to do with it.

Nevertheless, refusing to listen to the voices of caution and still believing that any publicity was good publicity, Secunda had several copies printed, with the band's name at the bottom. Somebody was rash enough to post one through the door of 10 Downing Street. Wilson did not send anybody out for a copy of the single, but sued for libel instead, obtaining an interlocutory injunction which forbade members of the band from talking about it, releasing it or distributing any further copies. To this day, those involved are still barred from speaking explicitly about the content, and the offending image has never been legally reproduced in print.

The first inkling that the band had of something being wrong was when black limousines started following them home. Their unease was confirmed when they arrived at a gig one night, Secunda showed them the card, hustled them into a dressing room, explained what had happened and told them to let him do the talking when they faced the press. Next day they were in a solicitor's office, where they were told to pose for photographs outside the law courts. When the storm broke, the band were staying in a hotel. One morning Carl was lying in bed, when Ace came in and dropped a collection of newspapers with lurid headlines on him, telling him to read them. Meanwhile, he declared, he was going to leave the country. In the end he never did, but he was annoyed about the libel on Wilson as he knew that his grandfather, who had been a member of the Labour party since its early days, would be furious.

The rest of the band were similarly fearful for the consequences. Echoing Ace's reaction, Bev said they thought they would definitely have to flee abroad and lie low. The case went to the High Court where Quintin Hogg, QC, said for the prosecution that the postcard publicising what he quaintly described in court as 'a song and dance number' amounted to 'a violent and malicious personal attack' on the Prime Minister. There was a further irony in that Hogg, a Conservative MP, had briefly been a candidate for the leader of his party four years earlier, only a few months after Wilson had become leader of the Labour party.

At the conclusion of legal proceedings on 11 October The Move were ordered to apologise, observe the terms of the injunction, hand over damages and pay all royalties from *Flowers* to be held in charitable trusts and shared between two charities of Wilson's choice, the Spastics Society and the amenity funds of Stoke Mandeville Hospital, as well as be liable for all legal costs. As one of The Move's most popular singles, and probably their most-played oldie on the radio ever, over the forty-plus years since it has amassed substantial royalty payments on airplay alone. The loss of these hit the group and particularly its writer dearly. In spite of this they still never managed to persuade Wilson's rival Edward Heath, leader of the opposition, to guest on organ with them.

The affair inevitably led to an intolerable strain in relations between them and Secunda, who was the man solely responsible for the fiasco. Frightened of what his next trick might be, The Move parted company with him. He claimed that he was bound to get in trouble again, but nobody was going to stop him from being a millionaire. Not with him, was the band's reaction. However, with his reputation as a tough albeit sometimes misguided manager, he was unlikely to be short of clients in future, and he later worked at times in a similar capacity for T. Rex, Steeleye Span and Motorhead among others. After this he moved to California, where he founded a literary agency and died after a heart attack in February 1995, aged 54 – coincidentally, just six days before lymphoma claimed the life of Denny Cordell at the age of 51. According to Don Arden, who replaced Secunda as their manager, he was furious when The Move dispensed with his services, took it personally and told everyone how he was going to 'do' Arden. The latter claimed that Secunda was 'totally wrecked on drugs the whole time' and ultimately died by his own hand, although his memoirs appear to be the only source for this last statement.

Lemon Tree had also been recorded by the Idle Race. Roy played guitar on the session, and it was scheduled to be their first single. But The Move's version, earmarked for their forthcoming LP, being on the B-side of *Flowers*, and attracted such heavy airplay that the Idle Race thought they would be seen as a covers band, as well as competing against their mates. They instantly withdrew their version from British release.

In November and December The Move took part in a 15-date package tour headlined by the Jimi Hendrix Experience, with Pink Floyd, Amen Corner, the Nice and Eire Apparent also on the bill, starting at the Royal Albert Hall, London, then playing at venues in Bournemouth, Sheffield, Liverpool, Coventry, Portsmouth, Brighton, Newcastle and other cities, winding up at Green's Playhouse, Glasgow. Their 30-minute set on the tour included *I Can Hear The Grass Grow*, the next single *Fire Brigade*, Tim Rose's *Morning Dew*, and up to three Byrds numbers, namely *Eight Miles High, So You Want To Be A Rock'n'Roll Star,* and *Why*. They were more fortunate than Pink Floyd, who as Bev recalled some years later had the unenviable task of opening the shows and only getting to play their two hit singles, *Arnold Layne* and the summer Top 10 entry *See Emily Play*.

Roy in particular was overawed by the experience of touring with the guitarist who had quickly become one of his idols, and later he said that watching him sometimes made him feel like simply throwing his guitar away. Jimi, he remarked, 'was a gentleman, a real polite sort of guy', though he was having problems with his hearing, 'going a bit deaf sticking his head in the speaker cabinets,' so Roy volunteered to tune his guitars for him. They jammed together on occasion, a conglomeration which might at any time include Roy on bass, Trevor on drums, Steve Winwood on organ and Chris Wood, also of Traffic on flute. That no tapes were rolling at any such session, unless anybody out there knows otherwise, is posterity's loss. Jimi played *I Can Hear The Grass Grow* once after rehearsal (although, again, he never recorded it), said an ecstatic Roy, 'and it was brilliant!'

At the time, the Jimi Hendrix Experience were recording their second LP 'Axis: Bold As Love'. One night they were at Olympic Studios working on the album, and backing vocals were needed on one track, *You Got Me Floatin'*. Bassist Noel Redding and drummer Mitch Mitchell were unequal to the task, so they invited Roy, Ace and Trevor around to do the honours. Hendrix, whom Trevor called 'the undisputed star (who) changed the face of British music', would prove a major influence on The Move in another way. Trevor and Ace both had their hair permed in an Afro, in emulation of his style, courtesy of Ace's hairdresser wife. Trevor soon regretted the gesture, when he found out that his hair came out in lumps and it took him two years to grow it out.

This package tour had proved a better match than one earlier in the year. In the summer of 1967 The Move, Amen Corner and Tomorrow had been on a bill supporting Billy Fury. According to Keith West, Tomorrow's vocalist, 'God knows who booked that.' It was a real end-of-the-pier-type scenario with Fury attracting a considerably older age group than the other acts, and West's outfit decided they would get themselves out of the situation the best possible way. They played so loud during the first set that Fury's manager, Larry Parnes, warned them that if they did not turn the volume down in the second set they would be thrown off. 'So we played even louder and got thrown off, and The Move went along with it as well and they got thrown off.' Amen Corner, however, toed the line.

Towards the end of 1967, The Move's second Regal Zonophone single was scheduled. *Cherry Blossom Clinic* was another cunningly commercial slice of pop-psychedelia, punctuated by more extravagant blasts from strings and brass by Tony Visconti, the end bearing a resemblance to the Beatles' *All You Need Is Love,* and Roy's wah-wah pedal guitar. With *Vote For Me* on the B-side, a song which took a few satirical swipes at the political world, acetates were pressed. But The Move felt they had had enough notoriety to last them a lifetime, and to release a single with lyrics about a lunatic asylum would be asking for further trouble at a time when they no longer needed any.

Instead they plumped for what at least one approving critic called the best song Eddie Cochran never wrote, *Fire Brigade*. One evening the band went back to the hotel after a gig in London, and Carl told Roy he had just learnt that they were due in the studio next day as they needed to record a single. Did he have one? Roy's reward for answering no was to be handed a bottle of Scotch and the key to one of the hotel rooms – and instructions to get on with it. By 8.30 a.m., nine hours later, the brand new and just finished song was ready to be played to the group. In his words, they had to 'hold him up' to complete the session as he was so exhausted.

Roy had long since proved himself as a dependable songwriter, able to deliver the goods whenever the group needed another hit. He was happy with this role, shunning the limelight and remaining something of a background figure, even remarking that he would have been content with a role similar to that of Brian Wilson in the Beach Boys, writing and producing while the others remained the focus of attention. Like Syd Barrett and Marc Bolan, childlike fantasies, post-war comics and the world of Walt Disney had provided inspiration for some of his stories in earlier days and would continue to do the same for much of his lyrics.

More mundane matters of general organisation would be left to the others, particularly Carl. The latter would relate that Roy needed a perpetual kick up the arse. When the singer arrived at the Wood household early one morning as the band had to fly out on a tour of Denmark, Elsie would urge him not to wake Roy, who was still asleep in bed with his clothes on. A tour abroad was arguably more important than a lie-in, and a little later they would be halfway down the M1. Only then would Roy suddenly and sleepily announce that he had left his passport at home, as the others gritted their teeth for a lightning dash back so he could go and collect it.

The first few months of 1968 were remarkable for the unanimity of the British rock scene in trying to pretend that flower power never really happened. It was no coincidence that the Beatles went back to straightforward rock'n'roll on the single *Lady Madonna*, and the Stones likewise ditched the hippy trippy aura of their previous single and album, returning to their roots on *Jumpin' Jack Flash* a few weeks later.

Roy also anticipated this return to basics from psychedelia, for *Fire Brigade* predated them both. Musically, and lyrically, it was a tour de force. Apart from the intro fade-in sound effects, it was entirely vocals (with Roy on lead for once), guitars and drums, with a snappy lead line and two-note bass riff borrowed from *Summertime Blues*. About eight years later, this same riff inspired Glen Matlock of the Sex Pistols when they were recording *God Save The Queen*. As with the previous Move singles, it was quite complex, boasting several different chords and a middle section. The words were a clever innuendo linking the tale of a schoolboy crush with veiled references to a building burning – recalling that time when the fire services had to put out a conflagration at the Marquee when smoke bombs got out of hand. An initial recording in November 1967 featured Matthew Fisher of Procol Harum on piano, but it never saw the light of day until The Move's 4-CD 'Anthology' 41 years later. Another take of the song made it on to vinyl, was released in January, and was a rapid seller, entering at No. 22 in its first week (the best debut performance by a Move single ever), rising to No. 10 next week and eventually peaking at No. 3.

It was quickly followed by The Move's debut, self-named LP, recorded over 14 months and released in April 1968. If you believed everything that you read in the papers, you would have learnt that early the previous year the master tapes for their first album had been stolen from a car and never returned. Like a number of other stories, it was another publicity stunt – anything to get more news coverage. With its striking front cover design by The Fool, previously responsible for creating artworks for the Beatles, of a psychedelic Catherine wheel on the sleeve, it contained three non-originals, Eddie Cochran's *Weekend*, Moby Grape's *Hey Grandma*, with Nicky Hopkins on piano, and the doo-wop oldie *Zing Went The Strings Of My Heart*, featuring a rare vocal from Bev.

The other ten tracks were all Roy's songs, including both sides of the last two singles, and *Cherry Blossom Clinic*. Among the rest, *Useless Information* was a gently cynical look at the human thirst for everyday trivia, a love-hate commentary on British character in the tradition of the Kinks' Ray Davies; *Yellow Rainbow* with its ecological theme of 'nature's struggle to survive' perhaps the nearest they ever got to a song with a message, and with Trevor on lead vocal; *Kilroy Was Here,* written around the American catchphrase which had become popular around the time of the Second World War; and *The Girl Outside,* a haunting ballad backed with string quartet, drawing obvious comparisons with the Beatles' *Eleanor Rigby*. This and *Mist On A Monday Morning,* which featured Roy singing to an accompaniment provided by the string quartet, harpsichord by Nicky Hopkins, and recorder by Tony Visconti, were forerunners of some of his early solo work and in a sense his work with ELO. *Walk Upon The Water,* a psychedelic-flavoured song which ended with an unusual coda of hunting horns, had been under consideration as the third single. *Vote For Me* stayned in the can and would remain unreleased until 1997, when it appeared on the first of several compilations which benefited from the CD era. Like the singles to date, the album was produced by Denny Cordell, with strings, brass and woodwind by Visconti. It sold respectably, reaching No. 15 in the LP chart.

Among tracks which failed to make the album were two more songs written by Roy, the uptempo Stax-style *Move,* which had been earmarked for a while as the B-side to *I Can Hear The Grass Grow,* and the Tamla-influenced *Don't Throw Stones At Me,* which featured Ace on vocal. Both eventually appeared on the digitally remastered fortieth anniversary of the album in 2008.

But by now, internal disharmony was beginning to drive The Move apart with personal differences and was rivalry in the studio over who was doing what. As Roy was writing all the original material, it was hardly surprising that he was gradually taking over lead vocals. Carl felt he was not getting his share as original front man, while Trevor and Ace, both of whom contributed occasional lead vocals, were demanding more of a say in the choice of material.

The first personnel change was not long in coming. Ace was increasingly growing apart from them. Sometimes they would pick him up in their van, drive to a gig and take him back without him having said a word to anyone. The only time he opened his mouth was on stage. In retrospect, Bev admitted that he must have been having personal problems, but in a bunch of 'hard-nosed Brummies', there was unlikely to be much sympathy going around. Roy thought him 'a strange person – very aggressive', who was fighting much of the time with Trevor.

In retrospect, Ace saw much of the problem as arising from the fact that some saw him as the star of the show. When Secunda and his business partner Rikki Farr came to see them in the early days, the latter told them they were a great band, but they needed a central figure. As far as he was concerned, their blonde-haired bassist was the one. Sometimes known as 'Ace The Face', he was good-looking and popular with the girls, in itself sufficient cause for resentment among the others. In his words, that was the afternoon The Move split up, when the rot set in. He felt that he had in a sense been separated from the others, each of whom wanted to be the star of the show. After they began having hits he bought an acoustic guitar and began writing himself, and wrote *William Chalker's Time Machine*. Had the song been recorded by The Move, it would undoubtedly have increased his stock considerably. For various reasons they passed on it, and it was recorded as a single by the Lemon Tree, whose line-up included Mike Hopkins and Keith Smart. It was released early in 1968 and produced by Trevor with Amen Corner front man's Andy Fairweather-Low but significantly, perhaps, Ace was not invited to participate.

By this time, he had become the Syd Barrett figure of The Move. He was at odds with teen adulation, having his clothes torn and hair pulled out by fans in the streets, even having scissors stuck in his eye – and despite being in a band with several major hit singles to their credit, still on the same money as they had while they were in the Vikings. While they were touring with Hendrix, animosity between him and the others was increasing. Various members in turn were going into the office, saying either Trevor or Ace, or both, had to go.

Unable to cope with the demands of being a celebrity, and his intake of drugs, he had a nervous breakdown. Unlike Syd Barrett, he insisted, he always delivered the show, even if he was on another planet. A Pete Best kind of situation developed, until at a rehearsal with them in March 1968 he took his bass off, threw it against the wall, and stormed out.

Trevor then switched from rhythm to bass guitar. After a few months recuperating from his experiences, Ace formed a new band, the Ace Kefford Stand, with Cozy Powell on drums. Released as a single on Atlantic in the spring of 1969, their cover version of the Yardbirds' *For Your Love* failed to chart. Another shortlived band Big Bertha, and a brief return to the music scene in 1976 with another band Rockstar, yielded only one single each.

In 1994 he gave his first interview to the press since leaving The Move when he spoke to Alan Clayson, and the results appeared in *Record Collector* that summer. He gave his full version of how the group had formed and gradually unravelled, the highs and the lows, the petty rivalries, his odyssey and battle with drugs in the years that followed, and how his bassline had been a major ingredient in *I Can Hear The Grass Grow*. Bill Wyman, whose bass riffs had been an integral part of the Rolling Stones' *Paint It Black* and *Jumpin' Jack Flash* to the extent where a co-writing credit would probably not have been unmerited, would undoubtedly have sympathised with him. To some, Ace was not only another Syd Barrett, he was like another Brian Jones, another Peter Green. Happily, like Green, he did eventually return to the music scene, and in 2003 he released a CD 'Ace The Face', consisting largely of the material he had recorded shortly after leaving The Move. Several of the songs were self-penned, and among the few cover versions was the Paul Simon song *Save The Life Of My Child*, featuring Jimmy Page on guitar.

While *Fire Brigade* was climbing up the charts, the band – evidently forgiven their previous transgressions - returned to the Marquee on 27 February 1968 to record what would eventually emerge as a live five-track 33⅓ rpm EP, 'Something Else From The Move'. Like a number of outfits who were finding regular success in the charts at around this time, the more commercial singles which were safe enough to fit into the radio playlists were not really that representative of their more heavy rock sound onstage. They regarded themselves as a Jekyll and Hyde band, and they were surely not the only ones. Playback revealed the original recording of the EP to be blighted by major distortion, and they returned on 5 May, by which time they were down to a quartet, to record again. Once more the recording equipment let them down, and left them with little alternative but to book a session in the Marquee Studios in Dean Street to re-record one-take live vocals.

Released in June, it comprised *So You Want To Be a Rock'n'Roll Star*, Love's *Stephanie Knows Who*, Eddie Cochran's

Something Else (of course), Cliff Richard's *It'll Be Me*, and Spooky Tooth's *Sunshine Help Me*, the last comprising a nod to Frank Sinatra's *Strangers In The Night* during the guitar solo. Made long before live LPs became the norm, it reflected the growing divergence between their stage act and their lavishly-arranged studio work. The EP had been common in previous years, but by now it had almost ceased to exist. Not until the maxi-single craze of 1970-71, and the rebirth of EPs proper in the mid-70s, did it become widespread once more. *Something Else* was soon deleted, and tracks never appeared on Move compilations until 1981, as the master tapes were missing. They were later recovered, and thanks to 21st century advances in studio technology, *Flowers In The Rain, Fire Brigade, Piece Of My Heart, The Price Of Love,* and *(Your Love Keeps Lifting Me) Higher And Higher,* recorded at the same time, were later released on 'Anthology'.

'Something Else From The Move' featured a much more raw sound, some distance from the beautifully crafted studio creations which characterised much of the album. According to Trevor, it proved that the band were 'natural rock'n'rollers', with the West Coast covers and Roy going wild on the wah-wah pedal. In Bev's opinion, it caught them as they really sounded onstage, while when The Move topped the bill over the Byrds at a subsequent Royal Albert Hall gig, guitarist Gram Parsons told them their version of *So You Want To Be a Rock'n'Roll Star* was better than theirs had been.

On 31 August The Move were among acts who played at the first Isle of Wight Festival. A crowd estimated at 10,000 came to see and hear a line-up which also included Fairport Convention, The Crazy World of Arthur Brown, The Pretty Things, Orange Bicycle, while topping the bill was Jefferson Airplane.

It coincided with the release of The Move's fifth single. Denny Cordell, Trevor had thought, failed to capture the energy of the band in the studio, and 'took the toughness out'. Yet Cordell's last work with the group was perhaps a little more tough than anybody had bargained for. Ever since *Wild Tiger Woman* appeared, opinions have always been sharply divided. Cordell had just returned to America so it was released as a rough mix, but even so, on the positive side, it was a new and heavier direction for them with its inventive guitar work and frantic pace. For Trevor, it was taking them along a less pop path, closer to 'the wild rock'n'roll' they should have been playing all along, and he expected it to give them their first No. 1.

But his was a minority view, for some found it noisy, lacking in melody and lyrically offensive, especially with lines like 'she's tied to her bed, waiting to be fed'. ('Just a bit of poetic licence,' said Roy, when questioned about the bondage aspects). When Tony Blackburn featured it as a newspin on his Radio 1 breakfast show, he made his disdain for it clear. On air he said he thought it was so appalling that if it had not been by a big name group, it would never have been played.

Its failure seemed to suggest that he had hit the spot, albeit rather harshly. Roy had been uncertain about its potential as an A-side, as were Bev, who said it sounded more like a album track and Carl, who remarked that his mother had liked their previous singles but definitely not this one. Each of them later said it was the wrong one for an A-side, and punters evidently agreed. To compound the issue, there were internal problems between management and label, which impacted adversely on the record's promotion. Whereas previous Move singles had all made the top five, this time it never even dented the Top 50. (According to the chartwatch.co.uk website, which aims to give all chart positions reached by every single and album to make the UK Top 10 since 1952 but also includes a few which fell some way short of such heights, it spent three weeks in the Top 60 in August and September, at 53 – 56 - 54 before disappearing right off the radar). In retrospect some thought the more tuneful *Omnibus*, the B-side, would have been a wiser choice. That is to say, if authorities at the BBC had not listened too closely to the lyrics, which to the casual listener might appear to be going for a ride on a public service transport vehicle and getting off at the end of the terminus, but could perhaps equally well have been taken (or intended by the crafty wordsmith) as a euphemism for more carnal activities.

Chastened by their first complete flop, the group's arguments about musical direction intensified. Disenchanted with the more poppy aspects of their sound, Trevor wanted them to go more decisively in the hard rock direction. After having been jamming with the likes of Cream and Steve Winwood, he had shared a flat with Noel Redding, Jimi Hendrix's bassist, with whom he had discussed the possibility of forming another band after the

Experience went their separate ways. In this he clashed with Carl, whose musical ideas seemed to lie in the opposite, more mainstream direction. If the next single failed to sell, they suggested, they would disband.

Denny Cordell was now concentrating more on his latest protégé, the former Sheffield plumber and gas fitter turned gravel-voiced soul man Joe Cocker. Skilled producer as he was, Tony Visconti felt that Cordell was only really a 'singles man', unsuited to working on albums. The Move thus had to seek a new pair of hands for the job and turned instead to Jimmy Miller, whose recent track record included hits for the Rolling Stones and Traffic. Playing safe, they came up with the much more radio-friendly *Blackberry Way*.

By this time the friendship and professional relationship between Roy and Jeff Lynne was blossoming, and both used to visit each others' homes to raid record collections and make demo recordings. Jeff was one of the first people in the area to acquire a Bang & Olufsen tape recorder with a sound-on-sound facility, enabling musicians to overdub additional instruments and vocals to their heart's content, or rather, as Jeff explained cautiously, 'until there's so much hiss you can't hear anything.'

Roy had long enjoyed experimenting with two tape recorders, transferring from one to the other and building up the sound a little each time. With the B & O recorder, he said, 'you could actually multi-track on it – but only so far. Myself and Jeff used to get to a point where you'd multi-track so much that you could see through the tape!' Thus armed, they worked on a demo of *Blackberry Way* at Jeff's house, beginning work one afternoon and working on arrangements as the hours raced by, until about 1.00 a.m., by which time the family were fast asleep upstairs. 'I had to kneel on the floor holding the mic, singing it,' said Roy, 'and Jeff and the drummer from the Idle Race, Roger Pritchard, were holding a pillow around my face while I was singing so Jeff's parents wouldn't be woken upstairs.' By this time they were all giggling so much that nothing but laughter could be heard throughout the last verse of the song.

Yet this resulted in the single that really changed The Move's style, as it was the first on which Roy had started doing his own demos, instead of going into the studio and explaining what he wanted. Laughter apart, the recording turned out very like the demo, and like *Fire Brigade*, with the writer on lead vocal. Hailed by critics as an affectionate pastiche of the Beatles' *Penny Lane*, with elements of *Strawberry Fields Forever*, Roy said that the lyrics evoked a picture of servicemen waving goodbye to their families before going off to the 1914-18 war. It featured mellotron and keyboards from fellow Brummie Richard Tandy, who had played gigs with them on keyboards and bass while Trevor was nursing a broken arm. Released just before Christmas 1968, it got them back on *Top Of The Pops* early in the new year. After entering the charts modestly at No. 49 in the Christmas chart it gradually picked up on sales, and in February 1969 it climbed to No. 1 for one week, the group's sole chart-topper.

On the B-side was *Something*, later retitled *A Certain Something*, in order to distinguish it from a slightly later and far-better known song by George Harrison. The Move's song had been the work of local songwriter Dave Morgan. Not a writer himself, Carl had gone into a business partnership with Trevor and set up the Penny Music Publishing Company, to promote the work of Morgan and Tandy, who were also working sometimes as a duo.

On the whole The Move were relieved to be back not only in the charts but also in public affection, and *Blackberry Way* went some way towards helping them pay off the ever-present libel action legal costs. But Trevor hated it, increasingly becoming the odd man out as Ace had done, and there were frequent rows between him and the others. At one gig while *Blackberry Way* was in the charts, he stumped across angrily to Bev mid-number, told him he was playing it wrong, slung his bass on the floor and stormed off. Bev furiously wrenched his hi-hat cymbal which had been screwed to the stage floor, and threw it after him. He ran off stage after Trevor as the curtain came down, and narrowly resisted the temptation to strangle him. When he declared that one of them had to go, Trevor immediately said he wanted out anyway, as he was sick of 'playing this crap.' Ironically, his departure meant that the two members who had originally started The Move in the first place had now gone.

Unlike Ace, Trevor continued to maintain a relatively active role in the music scene. It may have been a low key role, but as he often admitted, he never really wanted to be a pop star. He and Richard Tandy joined another long-standing Birmingham band the Uglys, with Dave Morgan on bass. The Uglys later changed their name to Balls, not a name calculated to get them played much on the radio. Session work at Island Studios and honorary membership of the Pink Fairies were also part of the picture. A drug-fuelled lifestyle in central London came close to catching up with him, until one night a deeply concerned Secunda turned up at his flat with a large bag of money, knocked on his door and ordered him to go back to Birmingham at once before he killed himself – an instruction he fortunately obeyed. Like Ace, Trevor's own songwriting talents, while never as prolific as those of Roy, had been hidden under a bushel for too long. In 1972, his *Down Down Down* was recorded as a single by Dave Edmunds, and despite not charting, it remained in his live repertoire for years. Eventually the Uglys became the Steve Gibbons Band, whose finest moment came when their version of Chuck Berry's *Tulane* made No. 12 in the summer of 1977.

The Shadows had disbanded at the end of 1968, and The Move made headlines again when they asked Hank Marvin to join them. To the music press, this hardly made sense. How could Britain's most respected pop guitarist possibly join this much younger bunch of controversial upstarts? It conjured up visions of Carl promising to leave his axe behind in the woodshed, and Bev swearing he would use his cymbals only for their intended purpose in future. When questioned years later, Carl said the invitation to Hank was nothing more than yet another publicity stunt, but Hank had by then confirmed that an approach to him was made by Roy Wood, who was ready to move to bass. He declined, apparently as he thought The Move's schedule would have been far too hectic for him.

Instead the group filled the bass vacancy with Rick Price, a friend of Roy from some years and guitarist with Birmingham band Sight and Sound. Among his earliest memories of being a member of the band were appearing on *Top Of The Pops* and *Lift Off With Ayshea*, wearing a shirt borrowed from Roy, and a pair of Carl's trousers and shoes but, he swore, his own hair and teeth.

Now Rick was a member, said Roy, the band seemed 'more acceptable'. Trevor had always been 'a bit outrageous on stage', while Rick was more a John Entwistle type, standing in the background while filling the bass and backing vocals role without trying to be the focus of attention. Carl put it a slightly different way when he said that with Trevor went the last vestige of anarchy in the band, though by this time The Move were trying to live the anarchic aspects down. The 'hard, aggressive band' image which had been foisted on them in the days of incidents at the Marquee and of the postcard was one with which they felt increasingly uncomfortable.

This was reflected in their changes of management. Having disengaged themselves from Secunda, they chose to go with Don Arden, who had previously looked after such acts as Gene Vincent, the Nashville Teens, the Small Faces and Amen Corner in addition to pursuing a very brief and very unsuccessful career as a recording artist himself as a balladeer in the Engelbert Humperdinck mould. While he did not specialise in publicity stunts, he already had a name for being a tough negotiator and for striking terror into the hearts of any rivals whom he feared were trying to poach his clients, as well as into any naive young musicians enquiring too closely into their business affairs, hence the nickname 'Don 'Ard 'un'. During an appearance on *Top Of The Pops* in 1969, an assistant to Peter Walsh, another manager, approached The Move to discuss whether they would be interested in working with him. When Arden heard of this, he and a few muscular friends paid an unannounced visit to Walsh's office. The latter was out at lunch at the time, and only Clifford Davis, then the manager of Fleetwood Mac, was there. He had his face slapped and was told that much worse would happen unless he laid off The Move. When Walsh returned and was told about the incident, he informed the police. They warned Arden that if anything happened to Walsh, he would be charged as the number one suspect. He admitted defeat and sold The Move's contract to Walsh, who also looked after The Tremeloes and Marmalade, and decided to put them on the cabaret circuit, a gesture undertaken more for business reasons than for motives of musical integrity.

Carl revelled in the idea of 'his' group playing to the scampi-in-a-basket set, and the easygoing Rick had been used to it in his previous group. Moreover, as 'the new boy', he was on wages and had no input, particularly in the business side of things, something he would soon regret. But Roy, looking ever more outrageous with his love of eccentric stage gear, shoulder-length hair and drooping moustache, cared little for this change of scene. However he and Bev, who disliked having to play his drums too softly, were both on the point of getting married, and cash was the prime consideration. With their wild reputation, it had been difficult for them to be choosy about their gigs, and cabaret would ensure a steady income. Becoming a cabaret band and playing songs like *Ave Maria* may have been sound economics, but it only increased The Move's dilemma as to whether they were a progressive rock band or an out-and-out pop group. They never fitted easily into either pigeonhole.

By 1969 the British music scene had become increasingly polarised. On one hand there were pop groups like the Tremeloes, Marmalade, Vanity Fare, Dave Dee, Dozy, Beaky, Mick & Tich, and the Love Affair, whose energies were directed almost entirely at the singles market. Their A-sides were generally written by others, and often used session musicians to some extent, and they had to be content with writing and playing the B-sides, although some of the Tremeloes' A-sides featured their own lyrics set to Europop melodies. On the other side of the fence was what the media labelled underground and progressive rock, personified by the likes of Deep Purple, Free, Black Sabbath, Ten Years After, Yes, Led Zeppelin, and Pink Floyd, all of whom who set their sights firmly on LP sales. Zeppelin and their management firmly refused to let their record company release their work on singles in Britain, although they had no control over such exploitation of their output in America and other overseas territories. Meanwhile the first four of those aforementioned groups caved in to pressure, issued singles in 1970 which were major hit singles, and were so dismayed to find themselves miming on TV shows and acquiring a teen following that they threatened to veto issuing singles forthwith.

Among younger bands, The Move were almost unique in having an uncertain foot in both camps. Roy Wood's songs were pop in that they made great singles - short, full of catchy hooks, and just right for the radio. But they were also characterised by clever production tricks and unusual instrumentation, initially Tony Visconti's responsibility but increasingly down to Roy's multi-faceted imagination. Far from being three- or four-chord verse-chorus, second verse-chorus affairs with a short instrumental break and final chorus to fade, they were cleverly constructed with extra little twists in the bridge, so much so that the average amateur guitarist generally had to know every major, minor and 7th chord in the Bert Weedon tutor and more, or read music, to have any hope of playing them. Very few of Roy Wood's songs used as few as three chords.

More than one observer compared his talents with those of the Beach Boys' Brian Wilson, and not just because of The Move's vocal harmonies. Both stamped their creative personalities individually on almost every track they made. Just because The Move and Beach Boys did and could make good commercial 45s did not mean that those records could not have deft little touches of detail and technique that showed how much their creators genuinely loved their work. But Roy was rarely hailed in the music press as a genius. And unlike too many of his peers, he had no need to dabble in dubious mind-expanding chemicals, his indulgences seemingly going no further than a fondness for vodka and red-hot curry.

When not earning their keep on the cabaret circuit while the swinging sixties tottered to a close, The Move pursued a bizarre double life as far as music was concerned. Their studio work, for the most part, was a confused hybrid of what they had to be live and what each of them wanted to play all along.

Only one new recording made it on to vinyl that year, the single *Curly*, released in June. The management's 'clean up The Move' campaign was in full swing, and something really poppy was required. *Curly* was notable for its absence of lead guitar. Weaving in and out of the vocals and folksily-strummed acoustic was Roy's multi-tracked recorder. Cheekily, it boasted very Beatleish vocal harmonies and a reference to Liverpool. Bev hated it, thinking it was pop at its most extreme. Roy likewise thought it was 'really corny' and he was not keen on the production.

Mike Hurst, a former member of the Springfields who had since then made a name for himself as Cat Stevens' first producer, and later went on to do the same for Showaddywaddy in the mid-1970s, was nominally at the controls. However the group put down their backing tracks and went to Olympic Studios to do the mixing. Roy waited around all day but Hurst did not turn up, so he decided he would mix it himself. It was a historic day, for in the other studio Roy saw the Rolling Stones recording what would be their most successful single ever in terms of British chart performance, *Honky Tonk Women*, produced (like *Blackberry Way*) by Jimmy Miller.

The single peaked at No. 12 that summer, proving that the group could no longer expect their new releases to go automatically into the top ten. However there had been some compensation a few weeks earlier when Amen Corner, another group with a teen following, who were yearning to make more 'mature' music, had enjoyed a No. 4 hit with Roy's *Hello Susie*.

It fared better than other songs Roy gave away around this time. The previous year, Cliff Bennett and his Band had recorded *You're Breaking Me Up (And I'm Wastin' Away)* as a single, released in April 1968. Some nineteen months later The Casuals tried to follow up their hits *Jesamine* and *Toy* with a Roy Wood composition, *Caroline*, which was not only produced by its composer but also bore the unmistakable sound of his backing vocals and quite possibly his recorder as well. Yet another, *Dance Around the Maypole,* was given to Acid Gallery, who had formerly been the Epics, while Roy produced and contributed vocals on the chorus, as did Jeff Lynne. Vic Elmes' lead vocal sounded not unlike it would if Roy had sung it, and without any exposure it sold so poorly that it inevitably became a collector's item. At one time rumour had it that it was actually Roy and some of the Tremeloes, probably as Acid Gallery drummer Mike Blakley was the brother of Alan in the Trems, under an alias. It was the only record ever to be released by the group under the name Acid Gallery, some of whose personnel left a few months later to form Christie, the *Yellow River* chart toppers.

A tour of the United States had been scheduled for January but postponed because of Trevor's departure. On 1 October, a cold autumnal morning, they flew out from England to New York via Boston for a long-delayed stateside jaunt, done very much on a shoestring budget. Far from being all articulated trucks and air-conditioned tour buses, it was the four band members plus John 'Upsy' Downing, the roadie, in a car with a U-haul trailer on the back full of gear. Upsy had been to America several times before in a similar capacity for Jimi Hendrix, but for the group, it was the first time they had ever been across the Atlantic. They were booked into a series of motels along the route, all sharing one family room, which generally housed one double, two singles and a camp bed. Two dates in Detroit were followed by a drive to LA along Route 66, then they had two days off in LA, where they played five nights at the Whisky on Sunset Strip, then had another long drive up to San Francisco for four nights at the Fillmore West, with Upsy and Carl taking turns at the wheel.

The physical exhaustion involved was bad enough without one incident of harassment on the way. Halting at a roadside diner bar in Texas, a bunch of rednecks objected to their long hair, a fight ensued and the group had to beat a hasty exit. An equally unwanted episode occurred when they reached LA and the hotel they had been booked into refused to admit them. They had to check into the Hyatt House on Sunset Strip, known as the riot house, where all the visiting bands stayed.

There had been nobody from their American label A&M to meet them on arrival, and when they found they had a day or two to spare in their itinerary, they visited the offices in Hollywood. When they arrived, nobody knew who they were, and eventually they were ushered into one of the pluggers' offices. Once they were all present, he pulled out a Move album from the bottom of a very dusty pile. They were not impressed by this unashamed lack of enthusiasm.

Nevertheless, as a virtually unknown quantity in America, they did not have to contend with the preconception of a top pop band which was known merely for a string of three-minute singles. Carl thought that this made things easier for them in the States than in England, as they 'seemed to end up with the image of a sort of rock'n'roll Byrds and we aren't complaining about that! They liked our records but didn't expect us to play them. They judged us on what we did on the night.'

Live recordings were made on two nights at the Fillmore West, where they shared a stage and dressing room with Little Richard and Joe Cocker, who were both also on the bill. A poor quality recording of *Open My Eyes*, a Todd Rundgren song, appeared on 'Omnibus', a widely-circulated vinyl bootleg issued in the 1970s. According to the typewritten notes and credits on the back, it appeared on Melvin Records, 'a non-profit organisation (but we didn't plan it that way), with an address 'c/o Harry Wilson, 10 Downing Street', and was dedicated to Roy Wood 'who is still a genius even if fate does its best to make sure no one finds out'. Not to be confused with a legitimate late 1990s compilation of A- and B-sides using the same title, the 'Omnibus' bootleg did not include the song of the same name, but also featured mainly live tracks, including the full output of the 'Something Else' EP, plus six numbers from a 1967 concert in Sweden, including *Flowers in the Rain, I Can Hear The Grass Grow, Hey Grandma,* and the Byrds' *Why*. The same recording, properly remastered, was given a legitimate release on 'Anthology' in 2008, alongside another cut from the same gig, a ten-minute version of *I Can Hear The Grass Grow*, interpolating riffs from *Night Of Fear/1812 Overture*, *Peter Gunn*, and at one stage threatened briefly to break into *Born To Be Wild*.

Carl was rightly proud of their performances, and he kept the tapes in the hope that one day all of the technical shortcomings would be cleaned up and made worthy of legitimate release in full. Sadly he did not live to see the day, but early in 2012 'Live At The Fillmore' was issued on CD. In addition to the two tracks premiered on 'Anthology', included were performances of *Don't Make My Baby Blue, Cherry Blossom Clinic Revisited, The Last Thing On My Mind, Fields Of People, Goin' Back, Hello Susie*, and another Todd Rundgren song, *Under The Ice*.

One night Rick's drink was spiked on what would be his one and only acid trip. After the gig he suddenly felt unwell, so Upsy offered to run him back to the hotel and return later for the others. When they appeared, he was semi-conscious in the middle of what looked like a room which had just been burgled. In fact he had ransacked it, and was in the process of unwinding all of Bev's exposed film, much to the latter's irritation. When it was obvious that he was not about to calm down and let them go to sleep, Bev offered to knock him out. Roy and Carl decided that it would be better if they took him for a long midnight walk instead. The three of them went to a coffee shop and sat there for most of the night. Fortunately it had been the last date on the tour – although an American promoter was waiting for them at New York airport, ready to take them to play some shows at Fillmore East which had been cancelled. As Rick was no better next morning, they bundled him onto the plane where he slept all the way back to Heathrow.

After having donned the mantle of a hard rock act stateside, somewhere between The Who and American psychedelic band Vanilla Fudge, suddenly reverting to the tame environment of the northern clubs in England was not really to the taste of three of them. Although he had enjoyed the 'underground' band ethos in America, back home Carl was the only one who really felt at ease. From one point of view Rick thought things could hardly be better, 'on great money, appearing in magazines and TV'.

But nobody was letting on that Roy and Carl were finding it increasingly hard to work together. Most of their disagreements took place in private, and as the management company felt no responsibility towards Rick, he was generally the last to know. Yet some of the problems were self-evident. Roy's colourful appearance provoked audience taunts on the 'Where's your handbag' theme, and when not turning down the amps Carl would play on that. After coming back from America, he told the press that they proudly believed they had the biggest freak in the world in Roy Wood - until they reached Los Angeles and found he was lost in the crowd. Likewise his remarks to the press that 'Our music stinks' did nothing to endear him to the others. Soon he and Roy were barely on speaking terms. He repeatedly threatened to walk out, and the rest were hardly inclined to dissuade him.

According to Bev, the last straw came at a show one thoroughly depressing night at a Sheffield club. As the group walked on stage, one slightly drunken punter pointed at Roy, called him a poofter and told him to get off the stage. Like most gentlemen of mild demeanour, Roy could tolerate jokes against himself up to a point. But there was one insult which could not pass unchallenged. He made the man an instant present of his vodka and lime, still in the glass - and the effect, to coin a phrase, was shattering. It travelled at high speed and smashed on the man's head, splitting it open. He went wild and hurled his lager at Roy but it missed him and exploded on the stage. The bouncers, who had not seen Roy throw his drink, dragged the man from his seat, took him outside and beat the hell out of him.

That night's performance went ahead in an atmosphere of extreme tension, punctuated occasionally with restrained applause. Backstage afterwards, Carl was livid with the other three whom he accused of ruining 'his act'.

Roy remembered the episode a little differently. In an interview about ten years later, he said that the problem arose when Carl himself walked on in a white suit, and he, not Roy, was the one whose manhood was questioned by an idiot customer. Nevertheless he admitted to his patience being exhausted, throwing the glass at him and hitting him in the head. The enraged said customer and his mates then started throwing pint glasses at the band, and waited for them outside afterwards.

But there was more to it than this one isolated incident. Carl had long wanted to be a solo artist, although whether this desire had predated Roy's plans for ELO or not is a moot point. At any rate, he did not intend to be a part of the new band, and he realised there would have been no place in it for him. One day the band were being driven down the motorway when Roy and Bev told him that they were intending to finish The Move and concentrate on ELO instead. He asked them to let him keep The Move while they went into the new band. If they did so, he would try and bring Ace and Trevor back into the fold and let Roy write the songs for them – although Ace and Trevor had proved that they were capable of writing material themselves and would have doubtless wanted their piece of the action as well. When Roy told him that they would only keep The Move going until it suited them to drop it, Carl retorted that they were being selfish and threatened to sack them all. As this was not practicable, he decided that he would walk instead. While they were touring America, he made the decision to choose a suitable moment to leave sometime after their return. With increasing disagreements about musical direction, added to the fact that Roy was writing all the original material and singing lead vocals on it, being reduced to a backing vocalist much of the time was frustrating.

Many years later, in retrospect, Carl admitted that although in some ways his years with the group were 'a wonderful time', it was 'more hard work than anything.' Playing with The Move 'was never the greatest thing because with hindsight I don't think any of us were that happy or that settled or comfortable with what we were doing', which was probably the main reason they broke up. He believed that they were at their best before they ever made a record, and after Ace Kefford left, 'it started to go down the tubes'.

In January 1970, it was officially announced that Carl had left the group for a solo career. Not being a writer, and without a band to join, in his words he went back to being 'a jobbing singer', as he had been before The Move were formed. The band promptly turned their backs on the cabaret circuit, terminated their management with Walsh and returned to Don Arden's stable or, as he would put it, 'they came running back to me'.

One month later The Move's second, long-delayed LP was released. Recording on 'Shazam' had begun early the previous year. At one time, the plan was for the album to be a double set, perhaps including several songs by Richard Tandy and Dave Morgan. In the end, the concept was slimmed down to a single album, comprising one side of cover versions and one side of original material. Roy was not so prolific as usual on the songwriting front at this time, or perhaps in view of the songs he had passed on to other acts or else recorded as a soloist 'because he felt they were unsuitable for the band' for a project which would come to fruition a little later, was being more selective than usual, and there were disagreements about which songs were to be included. In the end, most of the tracks were unusually long as the band were lacking sufficient material.

Nevertheless, Bev said in retrospect that it was his favourite Move album – 'all those gorgeous harmonies draped over those hard rock arrangements'. He thought it was some of the best production Roy had ever done, with perhaps not surprisingly an excellent drum sound. It was probably too clean for Roy's taste, he thought, as he was not a particular fan of Roy's 'everything but the kitchen sink' production which was soon to become his trademark.

Roy, Carl and Rick were credited as joint producers of the album, 'in conjunction with Gerald Chevin' from Straight Ahead Productions. This was something of a compromise, though Roy was the one who had really started feeling his way into production and had therefore been asked by the management to take over. Rick said it was very loose, as there was no producer in charge to tell them what worked and what did not. Although this might have had its down side, the sessions were still great fun for him; 'we were in hysterics the whole time, especially Carl and I.' Roy's memories of the sessions were very different; he thought it was 'a miserable album' for them all. To him it was a reflection of their not being 'together personally as a band', and pulling in different directions. However, in retrospect it was the album which changed them from a pop group to, in the parlance of the day, an underground outfit.

With artwork by Mike Sheridan, showing all four members as Superman-style comic book heroes, the end result was a compromise between the different directions each was pulling in, it contained six mostly lengthy tracks, side one original songs from Roy, and side two cover versions. All but one had been featured as part of the set on their American tour. Linking some tracks were jokey impromptu street interviews, recorded off the cuff when Carl went to record some of his vocals live in the street outside Advision Studios, people gathered round and he pointed the microphone at some of them, asking one or two of them what they thought of British pop music.

Side one was much the better, with its heavy guitar riff-driven treatment (very different from Amen Corner's) of *Hello Susie*, the string quartet-accompanied *Beautiful Daughter* (the only one not played live on the US tour), arranged by Tony Visconti who also played bass, uncredited, and *Cherry Blossom Clinic Revisited*, shorn of its psychedelic setting and featuring a long medley of classical pieces from Bach's *Jesu, Joy Of Man's Desiring*, the *Chinese Dance* from Tchaikovsky's *Nutcracker Suite*, and from Dukas's *The Sorcerer's Apprentice*. Roy had much preferred *Beautiful Daughter* to *Curly*, and wanted to release it as the next single.

Side two's standards, the ten-minute *Fields of People*, originally recorded by little-known American west coast outfit Ars Nova, *Don't Make My Baby Blue*, a Barry Mann and Cynthia Weil song which had been a hit for the Shadows in 1965 and also recorded years before by Frankie Laine, and Tom Paxton's *The Last Thing On My Mind*, a song popularised by the Seekers after its appearance on their Top 10 album 'Come The Day', were padded out by guitar and sitar jams, a fashion for which the Beatles and Hendrix could equally be credited – or possibly blamed. A Paxton song which had become a folk club favourite was a strange choice for extended wah-wah solos, although Mike Bloomfield and Al Kooper's recent live LP 'The Adventures Of' had done much the same to Paul Simon's *The 59th Street Bridge Song (Feelin' Groovy)*. In this sense The Move were merely following fashion instead of anticipating it, in a determined attempt to bury the three-minute pop singles image and look for more respectable album sales instead.

The bass work was unusually inventive, something for which Rick was anxious to credit Roy, who 'had a magnificent ear for bass.' He would play Rick the notes on the lower guitar strings and the latter would copy him; they were 'more like parts for a cello than for rock bass guitar.'

Not surprisingly in view of the American tour, rock critics over there loved the record. In *Rolling Stone* John Mendelssohn described it as 'powerful, intricately structured and following, a brutally energetic rock and roll album.' Yet it was poorly promoted, commercially it bombed, and neither this nor subsequent Move albums would ever have any impact on the album chart on either side of the Atlantic. In a sense, it was frustrating for them that the critical respectability and album sales which they were seeking never materialised again. Hit singles were all very well, but by 1970 there was a growing feeling that bands who could only sell singles neither wanted nor deserved to be taken seriously.

However, in retrospect it hardly mattered. A new and very important chapter for the band was about to begin.

3. *WHISPER IN THE NIGHT*

Ever since The Move had recorded their first album, Roy had been increasingly frustrated by the limitations of a standard rock group line-up. He had taken to recording songs on his own, overdubbing all voices and instruments, which would soon see the light of day as his debut solo project. At the same time, he wanted to form another group capable of using additional instruments like violin, cello and French horn, and playing more experimental classically-orientated music on stage. But to bring such a project to fruition would require far more cash than they as a group, record company or management could afford.

Cherry Blossom Clinic, the song which might have been the group's fourth single, was in a sense the godfather of ELO. Roy had had the ideas for the string parts, but as he did not have the ability to write them out in musical notation, he had to rely on Visconti to do them instead.

'I went down on the day when the orchestra was actually recording,' he said, 'and Tony was conducting it. To hear my song played by an orchestra was something different – it was something weird, and brilliant, and that's what started me off on the road to get ideas for ELO.' It occurred to him that there must be other young musicians playing classical instruments, be they cellos, violins, French horns or anything else, who would like to play in a rock band. 'I think after those tracks had been recorded with Tony doing the orchestral arrangements, that's when I started to get bored with The Move, with the band, because I thought there was something more to it than that.'

There were two alternatives open to him. One was to develop the sound of The Move by adding these instruments and additional players. The other was to plan a new group under a totally different name, and use The Move – a name which now stood for a rather demoralised unit with too many changes of image during its short history – as a vehicle, hopefully making enough out of hit singles and gigs to finance the brainchild until the latter was big enough to take off under its own steam.

The other members did not share his enthusiasm. When he drew pictures of how his ideal orchestra would look, including one with a cello section at the front and a picture of Carl playing timpani, the rest of them thought he had 'gone raving bonkers'. Bev likewise felt it was too much of a risk to give up The Move in pursuit of this ambitious venture which could not be guaranteed to succeed.

Fortunately there was at least one other musician and friend in Birmingham who could see the potential. This was Jeff Lynne, who had replaced Mike Sheridan as vocalist and main songwriter in the disintegrating Nightriders, shortly to become the Idle Race. They specialised in a whimsical, quirky pop style, and had won much critical acclaim for singles such as *The Skeleton And The Roundabout* and *Days Of The Broken Arrows* which, as sharp-eared listeners would readily point out, bore an ever-so-slight similarity in part to the chorus of *Wild Tiger Woman*. Among their most ardent admirers were Marc Bolan of Tyrannosaurus (later simply T.) Rex, and radio presenters John Peel and Kenny Everett. Like The Move, The Idle Race played regularly on stage at the Cedar Club, and it was not long before Roy and Jeff became close friends. They met regularly for a drink and a chat at the Pack Horse in Shard End, and it was partly thanks to Roy's insistence that the Idle Race were given a chance to record their first album at Advision Studios in London, where The Move had also benefited from the facilities.

Perhaps because of their success as a live group and their failure to dent the charts one iota, they still had the reputation of a cult group. Jeff had been invited to join The Move after Trevor Burton's exit, but he refused, still hoping his band would make it one day. One year and more critically-acclaimed but non-charting singles later, a realisation of the fact that they never would be really successful, plus the departure of Carl Wayne, plus Roy's interest in starting something new and more interesting, brought Jeff into The Move. During the last few days of February he completed his live commitments with the Idle Race, and then jumped ship.

The rest of the band thought that Jeff was the spark that they in general, and Roy in particular, had needed all along. The latter now had a new creative foil to set a friendly challenge as regards writing original material, and according to Rick, Jeff's joining 'sent Roy in a completely new direction'. Roy agreed, welcoming the fact that they had two songwriters instead of one, and somebody whom he really rated as a writer. It could however be argued that he overlooked the fact that Trevor and Ace had been capable of writing songs for The Move if only they had been given the chance.

Thus did the new project gradually become more than a twinkle in a few sets of Birmingham eyes. First, it needed a name. During one of their initial conversations, they discussed the possibility of having a large light show on stage like Pink Floyd. That night as he went home, Roy thought about the BBC Light Orchestra, light in this case describing the style of music. If they were to include a light show, and they were using electric instruments as well as electric lights, why not call themselves the Electric Light Orchestra?

Meanwhile, as The Move rehearsed for their first post-Carl college and university dates, they had to function without their front man. Roy was the obvious choice, but he had been used to standing in the background playing guitar and adding backing vocals on stage. As one who disliked the idea of pushing himself, or even being pushed, into the spotlight, such a role suited him. Basically he was quite shy and self-effacing, ready to admit that he was not great at conversation and found small-talk difficult. 'If you look at photos of me in the early days, I'm always the one hanging back with my head down, more the musician than the frontman.'

Yet as the obvious lead vocalist as well as the lead guitarist, he could hardly have had it otherwise. For their next appearances on TV, promoting the new single *Brontosaurus*, beginning with *Colour Me Pop*, BBC2's shortlived precursor to *The Old Grey Whistle Test*, he donned a long coat made up of black and white triangles, made up his face to match and added a star in the middle of his forehead, fortified himself with a few vodkas. In his words he went on 'leaping around like a maniac', rolling around the floor and biting the neck of his guitar. The rest of the band, who had not been warned, were so amazed that they almost stopped playing. This was not the Roy Wood they knew.

Brontosaurus, a kind of heavy metal dance song with tongue-in-cheek lyrics, was built around an engaging guitar riff and ended up as a frantic rock'n'roll duel between slide guitar and Jeff's boogie piano. Musically, it was as far removed from *Curly* and *Beautiful*

Daughter as could be imagined, and some reviewers found it hard to believe it was by the same band. Roy's voice had seemingly undergone a total transformation, as he delivered the lyrics in a curious vocal that was half growl and half scream. For some weeks after release in March 1970 it seemed destined to disappear quietly, especially after unenthusiastic reviews from some journalists who evidently preferred The Move's more poppy sound. But an appearance on *Top Of The Pops* (where Roy's new look appalled the more staid middle-aged viewers) and plays on Radio 1's contemporary show *Sounds Of The 70s* helped boost it to No. 7 in the chart. The B-side, *Lightnin' Never Strikes Twice*, written by Rick and Mike Tyler, the real name of Mike Sheridan, with Rick on lead vocal, had been recorded shortly before Jeff joined.

It was their last record on the Regal Zonophone label, which underwent a change of name that autumn and re-emerged as Fly Records. Simultaneously, in September 1970, The Move signed a deal with EMI's new progressive label Harvest, as 'The Move performing under the name Electric Light Orchestra', with three albums plus singles over the next three years. This left them with one further single and LP to fulfil the Fly contract. The single was another heavy rock'n'roll epic, *When Alice Comes Back To The Farm*. Featuring similar instrumentation to 'Brontosaurus', plus Roy's aggressive multi-tracked cello, and an interesting tempo change or two, it was a fine record but despite a new release slot on *Top Of The Pops* it gave them their second total miss.

Although they were having mixed success in the charts at this time, The Move were still hugely influential as far as some of their contemporaries were concerned. In particular The Tremeloes, who were trying to shake off their pure pop image, were great admirers. Their bassist and co-writer Len 'Chip' Hawkes admitted that while they were recording their new album 'Master', he was often inspired by the principle of 'what would Roy Wood have done on this track', and his bass riff for their last top ten single *Me And My Life* was worked out with him very much in mind.

There was a further connection between the bands when the mellotron which had been used on the Beatles' *Strawberry Fields Forever* was deemed surplus to requirements at Abbey Road, and sold to Jeff Lynne, then still in the Idle Race. Jeff sold it to Hawkes for £500 at about this time, while he was working with The

Tremeloes on a soundtrack for the film *May Morning*, and he later presented it to the Beatles Museum in Liverpool.

Had Roy and Jeff had their way, The Move would have been consigned to history so they could concentrate full-time on ELO. They called a meeting with manager Don Arden and EMI Records, to see if they would be prepared for an album by the new band. EMI had reservations; The Move had been a very successful name for them, and insisted that they keep the old band going. Only then would they accept an experimental album by the new project as well.

Bev was still unsure about the eventual success of the ELO concept. He was regarded as the best businessman of the three, encouraging them to carry on with the tried and tested name as the best way to finance the new idea. Roy and Jeff, he said, were full of musical ideas, but reluctant to give sufficient thought to the more mundane, practical aspects, and on his shoulders fell the task of trying to organise the recruitment of other musicians and rehearsals, as well as getting money together to make it all possible.

Both the 1970 Move singles appeared on the subsequent LP 'Looking On'. Packaged, for the British market at least, in a sleeve with a picture of bald heads and no photograph of the band anywhere (the band were certainly not the baldies on the front), made up of completely original material, and recorded between May and August 1970, it was quite democratic in terms of writing credits. Four of the seven tracks were Roy's, two were Jeff's, and one marked Bev's debut. In some corners the general opinion remains to this day that 'Looking On' was The Move's lamest LP of all, a grim exercise in heavy metal bandwagon-jumping unrelieved by the spontaneous if corny humour of 'Shazam'. In Bev's words, it was 'a bit ploddy'.

But to others it was a more colourful work than its predecessor, arguably self-indulgent in places but lightened by Roy's inventive use of oboe and sitar in places as well as Jeff's two songs, the melodic *What?* (also the B-side of *Alice* and an early forerunner of ELO balladry), and the semi-jazzy *Open Up Said The World At The Door*. Bev's *Turkish Tram Conductor Blues* was a riff-orientated rocker in the 'Brontosaurus' mould, complete with saxes, described by the writer as 'the sort of thing the Wild Angels might like to play'. Perhaps strangest of all, the opening title track was based on heavy guitar riffs and solos, broken up by sweeping piano interludes and a vocal which sounded more like Black Sabbath's

Ozzy Osbourne than Roy Wood, and then turned into an instrumental with jazzy guitar, sitar and oboe. (The sitar was not the Indian instrument as used by Ravi Shankar and other musicians from the same country, but a Coral electric sitar which was developed and manufactured in the late 1960s, in effect an electric guitar modified with a buzz bridge and extra strings on the body). The effect was like a song and instrumental merged together, both with different tempos. If 'Shazam' had raised any doubts about The Move still being a pop group, this record surely killed them altogether.

The album's longest track, *Feel Too Good*, was a nine-minute marathon that started out as a studio jam with Jeff, not Bev, on drums. For years, in the absence of a sleeve credit to the contrary, it was assumed that the backing vocals must have been Roy doing an impression of the Ikettes. Once one had a reputation for impersonating Dusty Springfield on stage, it was hard to live down. Only when the album was remastered and repackaged for CD release with bonus tracks in 2008 was it revealed that P.P. Arnold, a onetime singer with Ike and Tina Turner who had enjoyed Top 20 success as a soloist in 1967 with Cat Stevens' *The First Cut Is The Deepest*, and Doris Troy, were responsible. It was followed by a short hidden track, *The Duke Of Edinburgh's Lettuce*, a charmingly absurd snatch of doo-wop which then went into a singalong around the pub piano. Like the Beatles' *Her Majesty* on 'Abbey Road' a year previously, it could not be listed on the sleeve because of rules governing titles directly concerned with living royalty, though such restrictions no longer remained when the record appeared on CD many years later.

A further song written by Jeff, *Falling Forever*, was recorded around this time and broadcast as part of a BBC radio session around this time but never made it to official release.

Bev thought the record suffered from their not having enough songs to start with, and also from their having to contend with 'Roy's never ending line of weird and wonderful instruments'. Such perfectionism rather tested his patience. The drummer would go out for a break to the cinema, and when he returned, 'Roy was still fiddling around with his cello part.' With some tracks, which he admitted to having found downright embarrassing, he would put the drums on afterwards, and had to play out of time to keep in with them properly. And when it came to promoting the record, he had to do all the interviews with the music press – but, having been less involved in the recording than Roy and Jeff, often had little idea what he was talking about.

Likewise it was the end of The Move as far as Rick was concerned. Roy and Jeff shared the production of the record, he said, 'and Jeff was never the underdog in any shape or form'. His feeling was that Jeff was writing a large number of songs and Roy was finishing off whatever was used for him. Jeff, he knew, had a plan, but he himself did not; 'I just played the bass and then went home.'

Again, 'Looking On' failed to sell in sufficient quantities to make the album chart. The second single's failure might have been a contributory factor, coupled with lack of promotion by Fly Records. The Move had announced they would be leaving the label anyway, and Fly's interest was in any case fully taken up with its flagship act, T. Rex. As Tyrannosaurus Rex the duo had been something of an underground cult act. They too had migrated from the Regal Zonophone label, had now shortened their name and were about to become the biggest name in British pop since the recently disbanded Beatles.

During the closing months of 1970, The Move were still playing live regularly. One such gig at Manchester in September was described in detail in a review of which was posted by a fan on the Move online bulletin 'Useless Information' some years later. Among the songs in the set were five of the tracks from 'Looking On', all but *Open Up* and *Feel Too Good*, alongside the Beatles' *She's A Woman*, *Lightning Never Strikes Twice,* and *I Can Hear The Grass Grow*. Calls for *Flowers In The Rain* and *Blackberry Way* went unheeded. Rick, it was noticed, did most of the talking between songs, and at one point he asked the audience to pause for a moment in memory of Jimi Hendrix, who had died the previous day.

Yet Rick's days with the group were drawing to an end, and by early the following year The Move had slimmed down to a trio, existing almost completely just on record and TV. Rick needed work to support his family and pay the bills, and after doing some work on solo projects he went off to form a new band Mongrel with vocalist and keyboard player Bob Brady, and drummer Keith Smart, formerly with the Rockin' Berries and Lemon Tree. The outfit had been formed mainly as the result of a call from Carl, who wanted somebody to back him on his new cabaret act. Although he sent tapes of songs and arrangements to be learnt, he never showed up for rehearsal. At length they grew tired of waiting, added a few self-penned numbers and took what would have been Carl's set on the road, with Brady taking most of the vocals.

Jeff was not keen on touring, and much happier working in the studio. Yet as far as EMI were concerned, The Move were still very much a force to be reckoned with in the charts. Of their nine singles to date, five had reached the top five, one of these had made it all the way to No. 1, and only two had missed out completely. However the interviews Roy, Jeff and Bev were giving to the music papers about their working on the launch of ELO made it obvious where their interest lay, with talk of a nationwide tour as soon as the right musicians to augment them could be found. It even reached the point where a *New Musical Express* reader, claiming to be tired of reading about it, wrote a letter which was published in the paper urging Roy to put an advert in the small columns for the right musicians and give everyone else a break.

The aim of the project, Roy said, was to break down the barrier between classical music and rock, by bringing them together for the first time. It had recently been tried by The Nice, who had disbanded early in 1970 and left keyboard player Keith Emerson free to form the classically-influenced trio Emerson, Lake and Palmer, and Deep Purple, whose classically-trained keyboard player Jon Lord had composed a *Concerto For Group And Orchestra*, first performed at the Royal Albert Hall in 1969. Both outfits had to acknowledge that in putting rock musicians at one end of the stage and the classical players apart, the fusion had only been achieved in part.

ELO had begun recording their debut album in the summer of 1970. *10538 Overture*, a song written by Jeff, had originally been intended as a Move B-side, but it soon took on a life of its own and was now talked about being the band's first single. The song, guitar and lead vocal clearly bore Jeff's imprint, but the cellos were just as transparently Roy's work. He was heavily into collecting and teaching himself to play various musical instruments at the time, among them a cheap Chinese cello.

After the four of them had recorded the basic backing track of the song with guitars and drums he took it into the control room while they listened to the playback, scraping away on it in *I Am The*

Walrus-type fashion. Jeff was so enthusiastic that he insisted they add it to the track there and then, and he ended up putting about ten cello parts, perhaps more, on the track. Meanwhile Bev and Rick had gone home, leaving Roy and Jeff to run riot in overdub paradise until, in his words, it sounded 'like some monster heavy metal orchestra'. Although Rick had played bass as usual, Roy later erased his work and substituted his own bass overdubs instead.

When they came to record the vocals between them, Jeff was looking for a title to portray a man with a number instead of a name. After staring into space for a while, they noticed the serial number on the modules of the recording console, 1053. An extra digit was needed to make it scan, and it ended up as 10538. They did a rough mix of the track, and both of them took a cassette home which they played non-stop for a while. While travelling to gigs to fulfil their last few bookings they were contracted to play as The Move, Roy and Jeff were demoted to the back seat, out of reach of the cassette player in order to try and prevent them from putting the track on yet again. They circumvented this by bringing their own portable cassette player with two speakers in the back, and played it again and again, 'to the point where it got up everybody's nose.'

From that Roy, Jeff and Richard Tandy, who were overseeing the project between them, gradually began recruiting additional musicians. The first were Bill Hunt on French horn and hunting horn, and Steve Woolam on violin, both of whom appeared on the first album, released in November 1971. Five tracks, including an extended version of what would be the eventual 45, *10538 Overture*, were written by Jeff. The remaining four were Roy's, among them an instrumental which was clearly not a million miles removed from Mason Williams' 1968 Top 10 hit *Classical Gas*, titled *1st Movement (Jumping Biz)*, the hymn-like *Whisper In The Night*, covered as a single the following year by Graham Bonnet of Marbles and later Rainbow fame, and *The Battle Of Marston Moor*, a cello-based instrumental preceded by speech from Roy impersonating Oliver Cromwell as he berated King Charles I. Bev thought that track was so awful that he left the drums to Roy on it.

To keep the baroque and classical theme going, the photos of Roy, Jeff and Bev in seventeenth-century costume were taken at the Banqueting House, Whitehall, alternately clustered around a large light bulb or posing with cello, violin and flute.

After the final gig as The Move, Rick Price said he would have to leave. As he had a family to support, he could not afford to give up live work. The three-piece, TV and vinyl-only Move, issued two singles and a final LP during 1971. As for the singles, *Tonight* was predominantly acoustic, with a capo on the fretboard to pitch it higher and a distinctive George Harrison-like lead guitar break. For some weeks it seemed destined not to chart, but thanks largely to its being championed by an enthusiastic Alan Freeman every Sunday afternoon for several weeks on Radio 1's *Pick Of The Pops*, it eventually took off and reached No. 11 in July. The follow-up *Chinatown*, a song with an Oriental flavour, had a B-side written by Jeff, *Down On The Bay*, and peaked at No. 23 in November.

At the same time, their final LP 'Message From the Country' hit the shops, and in the view of many it was their best. Gentle melodic songs by Jeff, like the title track (with undeniable melodic similarities to *10538 Overture*) and *No Time*, sharp rockers by Roy like *Ella James*, *It Wasn't My Idea To Dance*, *Until Your Mama's Gone*, were all thankfully free of the last two LPs' self-indulgence, with no tracks lasting more than five or six minutes, and there was a pseudo-Johnny Cash countrified song *Ben Crawley's Steel Company*, with Bev singing. On *Don't Mess Me Up*, credited to Bev as a writer, they did a clever impersonation of vintage Elvis Presley and the Jordanaires. *The Minister*, one of Jeff's songs, had more than a slight resemblance to the Beatles' *Paperback Writer,* while *Ella James* was released briefly as a single, but withdrawn in favour of the more commercial *Tonight*.

The band knew it would probably be their swansong, and so in Roy's words they just decided to have fun, experimenting and taking it easy. For him, it made the recording a very enjoyable experience. Jeff said it was 'all about experimentation, weird stuff and being silly', while Bev called it 'eclectic', and while naming it as probably his least favourite Move album, admitted that it did exude a sense of fun, 'which was rare at that time, with many other bands taking themselves far too seriously'.

Most of the bass on 'Message' was by Roy, in addition to the sax and woodwind instruments. Like the cello, which was not used on the album, he had lately developed a keen interest in the oboe so he could play it onstage when ELO began to start gigging. He was increasingly bored with playing guitar, and Jeff had now more or less taken over as the band's lead guitarist.

So in the studio, where did The Move finish and ELO start? Roy stressed that they were trying to keep both as far apart as possible. 'I write in two totally different ways for The Move and the ELO, always conscious of not putting strings on a Move record in case it comes out like the ELO, and keeping saxes out of the ELO.' The latter made their first performance in session for Bob Harris's *Sounds of the 70s* on Radio 1, recorded at BBC Radio Birmingham on 4 February 1972 and broadcast ten days later.

Meanwhile, in October 1971 The Move played their first gig in about a year. It would also be their last. A testimonial for long-serving Birmingham City footballer Ray Martin, it took place in the Swan pub, with the Idle Race and Raymond Froggatt also on the bill. With Richard Tandy, who had virtually become a member of The Move in their final phase in all but name, augmenting them on rhythm guitar, the group arrived on late and were greeted with a chorus of boos. They then delivered a set which included hits such as *I Can Hear The Grass Grow, Fire Brigade,* and *Tonight,* Jeff's *Down On The Bay,* plus covers of *Great Balls Of Fire* and the Beatles' *She Came In Through The Bathroom Window*. Around that time they appeared on the German TV show *Beat Club*, playing *Ella James*, on which they were also joined by Bill Hunt on piano.

In January 1972, a single was released by a supposedly new act, Grunt Futtock. *Rock'n'Roll Christian*, on the Regal Zonophone label, was produced by Andrew Loog Oldham, the former Rolling Stones' manager. Grunt Futtock were nothing more than a one-off wheeze created by Oldham and Don Arden, who put Roy, Steve Marriott of Humble Pie, former Humble Pie member Peter Frampton, and his fellow member of the recently disbanded Herd Andy Bown, later keyboard player with Status Quo, into a studio together to create the song. Arden later said he had no idea who was on the recording, which to him was 'a horrible, tuneless noise from start to finish', and thought it was probably Oldham playing around drunkenly in the studio on his own, but other sources suggested otherwise. A few photographs of art students who had nothing whatsoever to do with the record were taken in order to maintain the pretence of a band new band of unknowns, and EMI reportedly bought the record plus the non-existent band for £10,000. Like Acid

Gallery's *Dance Round The Maypole* some two years earlier, the single received zero airplay and disappeared without trace, only to achieve a posthumous distinction much later as one of the most collectable artefacts of its age. As for the identity of Bernard Webb, who was credited with writing the song, nobody was any the wiser. Whether it developed out of a jam by all the musicians together or was another of Roy's songs under a pseudonym was left to speculation.

What turned out to be the final Move release was recorded in December 1971 and hit the shops in April 1972. This farewell maxi-single was one of their best and among their most successful, putting them back in the Top 10 for the first time since *Brontosaurus*. The A-side, *California Man*, was a glorious Jerry Lee Lewis-inspired rocker with tootin' saxes, pounding piano, and Roy and Jeff sharing lead vocals on different verses. John Peel, who was the main keeper of the flame for anything remotely out of the ordinary for Radio 1 at the time and also the regular singles reviewer for *Disc and Music Echo,* wholeheartedly approved of it, though he admitted it did not have the tunefulness of some of Roy's work, and was not too hopeful about its chances of being a hit. Meanwhile his opposite number in *New Musical Express*, Danny Holloway, who in his column had only weeks earlier dismissed *When Gran'ma Plays The Banjo* as a slight, forgettable novelty tune only worthy of Ray Stevens and his ilk, could not contain his enthusiasm. He called it 'the most amazing single I've heard in ages', and at the end of the year he would nominate it as one of the best 45s of 1972.

On the B-side were *Ella James*, and another brand new track, Jeff's *Do Ya*. The latter became The Move's only US Top 100 hit and was later covered by Todd Rundgren. When Jeff incorporated it into ELO's stage act some time later, the only Move track to be thus honoured, reaction was so favourable that they re-recorded it on the 'A New World Record' LP in 1976.

By now the dual identity of both groups was at its height. Roy, Jeff and Bev would be dashing from the TV studio where they had been promoting *California Man*, Roy in Teddy Boy costume and long green coat, to play live as ELO. On stage, their repertoire included some songs from the first album, notably *10538 Overture, Queen Of The Hours*, and *Whisper In The Night*, as well as two lengthy epics written by Jeff from the second which they had just begun recording, both going under the working titles of 'Jeff's Boogies' plus a number, *From The Sun To The World*, and *In Old England Town*, Roy's tender *Dear Elaine*, which had been recorded as part of his still-to-be-released solo album, and a new arrangement of *Great Balls Of Fire*, with additional cello embellishments.

After a tour had been scheduled for March but cancelled as they had been unable to recruit the additional musicians required to reproduce the material in concert, ELO finally managed to convene the right line-up for that all-important first show. Their live debut was on 16 April at the Greyhound, Croydon, a venue which featured live progressive rock once a week.

An audience of about 400 (others estimated considerably less) came to watch, and sympathetic critics who wrote up the show in the music press admitted that this was something very new and innovative, but to an impartial observer the sound left much to be desired. They had plainly not found their feet, and in spite of optimistic interviews, early gigs were hardly spectacular. Roy was playing guitar less, using bass, cello, bassoon and oboe much more, and alternating between so many instruments on stage meant that his leads would invariably end up in a tangle.

Pioneers generally have a rough ride when it comes to technology, and in those days electric orchestras were some way ahead of what the amplification world could muster for them. There was no proper way of amplifying the instruments effectively, and the best they could do was to buy contact mics and jam them down the bridge of the cellos. The rhythm section had been used to playing loudly, and the string instruments could not match them volume-wise. When the contact mics were turned up, horrendous feedback was the result. Instead of having the cellos at adequate volume, they had to wear headphones so they could hear through one earpiece and hear the rest of the band as well. Sometimes the gaps between numbers which were needed to change instruments were almost as long as the numbers themselves, and once they came off stage afterwards, there would be arguments as to the volume of Jeff's guitar or the artistic merits of Roy's assorted collection. The combination of rock and acoustic classical instruments was a very novel concept in 1972, and experimenting in public to a paying audience was probably not the ideal place to do so.

On stage Roy was an almost ghostlike apparition, looking like Old Father Time with his long white wig, hiding behind little black glasses in a white wig, dressed in a monk's habit. For the promotional film of *10538 Overture* he whitened his beard with talcum powder. Unfortunately, as soon as he started singing, clouds of white powder (luckily everyone could tell from the scent that it was not the illegal sort) went everywhere. Next time he tried using Meltonian tennis shoe whitener, which stayed put – too well put, in fact, as it took about three days to remove afterwards. 'Oh well, anything for art,' he conceded. Yet from past experience, what he had considered to be good bands did nothing, as they had nothing to offer visually. ELO would not make the same mistake.

One mistake which was perhaps fortunately kept under wraps was when they appeared in a movie, *Freedom City*. To their relief, what might have been the most terrible picture of all time was started but never finished. A director called John Elton, whom they inevitably dubbed 'Dwight Reg', invited them to star in a film which was to be shot in around two weeks in the Barbican area of London. It was meant to be a science fiction with vague political overtones, with the album being used as a soundtrack, starring members of the group despite their total lack of previous acting experience. No script had been prepared beforehand, and the costumes were bus conductors' uniforms on loan from London Transport, except for Roy who had to make do with a long black coat with black and white flaps which he had worn on *Top Of The Pops*. Ever the lucky one, Roy's main role was to carry a rather well-endowed blonde up to the top of a flight of steps as she was supposed to be dead. She was wearing a very flimsy dress, which failed to preserve her modesty. As she was too heavy for him to carry with ease, they had to do repeated takes until he was unable to lift her any more. Jeff's sole line of dialogue came when he was meant to drink a glass of wine, glance to his right and say, 'Time to go.' He ended up getting the dialogue right, not difficult, but then turning his head and pouring the wine down his ear.

After the first week of shooting they were all invited to an office in Denmark Street, Soho, to look at the rushes, and fell off their chairs laughing at what they saw. It will all come clear in the end, Elton assured them, and that was the last they – or, so it seems, anybody else - ever saw of it.

As for the live music situation, part of the problem was in playing too many large venues too soon. If they had concentrated on small clubs at first, he was sure, they would have had time to get the sound together. But in the bigger halls, everyone turned up the electric instruments, and sometimes nobody could hear what the string players were playing. Footage from a gig at Guildford Civic Hall in May recorded by a member of the audience suggests that the negative reporting of early performances may have been exaggerated, but perhaps it was inevitable that there would have been good nights and not so good nights. Some shows were very poorly attended, particularly a gig at The Locarno, Sunderland, to which precisely seven punters turned up – an audience which was outnumbered by the band.

Yet the biggest obstacle to the band's well-being was probably the matter of having two leaders. As the better-known of the two, Roy was getting nearly all the media attention, which was unfair on Jeff as he had written the majority of their material. Roy Hollingworth's very enthusiastic review in *Melody Maker* in November 1971 had begun with the words, 'Oh Roy Wood, you've done it this time, you've really done it', which was all very well for one of its leading personnel but not the other. Don Arden thought that the trouble was a matter of Roy considering he was the leader, but Jeff was no longer prepared to tag along as he had been in The Move, because ELO was his group as well.

As soon as they came off stage, the cameras would invariably click in Roy's direction. A performance of *10538 Overture* on BBC-2 TV's *The Old Grey Whistle Test*, a late-night music show which sought to complement *Top Of The Pops* by giving exposure to artists who had released albums instead of focusing on new singles, was followed by presenter Richard Williams' remark on air, 'Great song, Roy.' As front man of the then leading rock programme on TV and a senior writer on *Melody Maker*, he should have done his research more thoroughly. It was symptomatic of the focus on one musician which was understandably resented by the other. (Old habits die hard. In the late 1980s, after he had left Kiss, Ace Frehley formed the band Comet, whose repertoire included their version of *Do Ya*, which he referred to in at least one interview around the time as a Roy Wood song).

To compound the issue, musical differences were beginning to emerge. Roy unwittingly gave away more than he intended in an interview with the music press at this time. His idea was for adding a brass section, in particular 'a row of saxes going like the old rock'n'rollers'. Such a concept seemed rather at odds with his and Jeff's ambitions for perfecting the fusion of pop and classical music. It was also a little ironic, given the view of Nigel Reeve, Director of Repertoire at EMI Records, that at the time Roy's ideas were almost completely orchestral, outside the rock'n'roll spectrum, unlike those of Jeff. Yet Roy was ever the restless one, always pushing the envelope out one way and then another. It was becoming increasingly obvious that both co-leaders had different musical aims within the band.

In an interview about twenty years later, Bev said that Roy did not do much for ELO, apart from having the idea to start it - arguably quite an important contribution, one might think - and thinking of the name. But in his view there was nothing of real substance on the debut album apart from *10538 Overture*. Significantly, many punters who would buy ELO albums in their thousands towards the end of the 1970s when they were among the bestselling British acts around would always find this first album a very acquired taste, if not downright unlistenable in places. Conversely, said Bev, Jeff never really did anything for The Move. With hindsight, perhaps he was a little less than fair regarding the contributions of each member to the 1971 Move and ELO albums on Harvest. Several long-term fans who followed the careers of The Move and the Idle Race, and all those within their ranks, from the beginning, have always liked and enjoyed the inventiveness of the first album.

Be that as it may, it was soon evident that one of them would almost certainly have to go. Everybody around them saw it coming sooner or later. Bev had assumed that when Roy and Jeff got together, they would collaborate on writing songs as a team. As the first album amply demonstrated, that did not happen. Rick Price, who had remained a close observer as well as friend, knew that while Jeff's encouragement had been vital for Roy in their getting the group together, there was a problem of egos. In The Move, Carl had had a big ego, 'but he would bite his tongue and make it work because it was business.' With Roy and Jeff, both accomplished songwriters and multi-instrumentalists, the rivalry was musical.

Mike Sheridan had observed the two of them at close range, and was convinced it was untenable. As he said, it was like witnessing 'two egos on a stick.' He saw an ELO gig at Selly Oak Town Hall, and in the process witnessed what almost seemed like a fight for who was coming on stage last. That Jeff's and Roy's songs were so very different only emphasised the gulf between them.

In order to try and resolve the issue amicably, the band decided to go to Europe for a while, and undertake a short and none too happy tour of Italy. This brought on a set of different issues. Journalists were still 'in Move mode', making it plain they only wanted to interview Roy. Although he explained as much as he could that the band was a team effort and he was not the sole leader, the frustration was getting to him and Jeff. The atmosphere between them was not only deteriorating, but also impacting on the performance and morale of the rest of the band. Moreover the main members had been under considerable strain to get the band together in the first place and to try and represent the sound of the album properly on stage, something they were still a long way from achieving. It all made for a rather fractious environment.

Don Arden recalled that at one sold-out show, an announcement was made that the group were unable to perform that night. Fearing that something terrible must have happened to one of them, he went backstage and found that Roy and Jeff were refusing to go onstage until it was mutually agreed which one would walk out first. He grabbed them both by the hair, shoved them out of the door and marched them on stage, threatening to beat the hell out of them if they didn't get on with it. They accordingly obeyed and the audience were ecstatic, but he noticed that neither of the two main men would even look at each other during the show. Afterwards they both went to see him separately in his hotel room and told him that they could no longer work together. He thought that Roy was the talented one, the one who had been coming up with the hits for years and would doubtless continue to do so, and that Jeff, who 'had always been just the other guy' could easily be replaced.

Roy thought in retrospect that the management had a responsibility to step in, take him and Jeff aside, and advise them to take a deep breath if not a complete rest. Instead, it seemed that they were encouraging and exacerbating the situation for their own ends. In his head, he suspected that his departure would only be a matter of time. Not feeling like he wanted to socialise with anyone else, he merely sat in his hotel room and wrote what turned out to be mainly the lyrics for songs which would appear on the debut album by the next band which he was beginning to visualise. Jeff and Bev could see which way the wind was blowing, and as Roy was still the best-known name among all three, they wondered whether he was planning to take the name ELO and leave them to continue as The Move.

From Roy's point of view, his friendship with Jeff was on the line, with the latter increasingly angry and no longer speaking to him. It was beginning to look unpleasantly like *déjà vu* after the personality clashes which had resulted in the departures of first Ace Kefford, then Trevor Burton, then Carl Wayne, from The Move. Having been through all that, Roy was disinclined to see history repeat itself.

Any hopes of their putting the bad vibes from that night in Italy behind them and making up again once they returned were soon to be dispelled. Matters came to a head again during a row between Roy and Jeff when they went back into the studio. Instead of taking a few days away from it all to cool off, they were under pressure to go back to work on the second album, on which Roy was playing bass more than anything else. Fuses were increasingly short, and when Jeff insisted he was playing it wrongly on one arrangement, Roy snapped at Jeff to play it himself, put the instrument away, and walked out.

Since leaving The Move, Rick had recorded a solo LP, 'Talking To The Flowers', in addition to forming his new band Mongrel. He had played bass on some of the early ELO sessions, although he regarded the project as something of a joke at first, and the contributions he had made on tape were erased. Nevertheless he was still an old mate, and it was him whom Roy went to see while pondering his musical future – a future in which he was determined to make a fresh start.

At the time *California Man*, a record by a now non-existent group, was ensconced firmly in the Top 10, spending three weeks at its peak position of No 7. Although The Move were still very much in the public eye as regulars on *Top Of The Pops* on Thursday nights, with the single being played regularly on Radio 1, Roy had left, and helped to call time on, that band to form another. He was now on the point of leaving that second outfit as well.

4. *SEE MY BABY JIVE*

After a period of rumour and uncertainty, and about a week after what turned out to be the final show played by the first line-up, at King Sound, King's Cross, London, the solution to the impasse was revealed at a press conference called by Don Arden at EMI House, Manchester Square, in July 1972. It was confirmed that in future Jeff would be taking full responsibility for ELO, which would also include Bev Bevan, Richard Tandy, Wilf Gibson, Mike Edwards, and additional musicians who would be auditioned. Roy was no longer involved and would be forming a new group with Bill Hunt, Hugh McDowell, and sound engineer Trevor Smith. Full details of the new outfit would be released shortly. Meanwhile, The Move would remain as it had been for the last three years, a recording-only outfit filling contractual obligations comprising Roy, Jeff and Bev.

Roy's new ensemble, which had been an open secret on the Birmingham music grapevine for a while, consisted mainly by the members of Rick Price's Mongrel. Rick Price filled the bass and backing vocal slot, and brought in drummers Charlie Grima and Keith Smart. With the addition of saxophonists Mike Burney, who had previously worked with jazz virtuoso Johnny Dankworth, and Nick Pentelow, plus Bill Hunt on keyboards as well as French horn, and cellist Hugh McDowell, the eight-piece line-up was complete and ready to spend the summer rehearsing in Roy's garage at his house. The initial idea for the sound was developed partly from a couple of tracks on his solo album, recently completed and still awaiting release, and partly from his vision of 'a modern John Barry Seven or Lord Rockingham's XI'. In time, though, others would see Wizzard as bearing predominantly the influences of Phil Spector and the Beach Boys.

With several former alumni of school- and college-educated musicians in the line-up, the band's leader and composer-in-chief had one serious disadvantage, but he had devised his own way of getting round the problem. 'I couldn't write music, so I developed my own musical code,' Roy said. 'I would write out the names of the notes, and if it was high I'd put a little circle over it, and if it was low, a capital "L". If I wanted the notes joined together, I'd do a wavy line under them. Luckily, the band soon became very good at reading it.'

Bill said later that friction in ELO had been inevitable at the top sooner or later, with two very talented and ambitious musicians, and it had come to a height on the Italian tour. Roy told him that he had had more than enough of that kind of atmosphere and tension with the original Move line-up, and had no wish to go through that again. Despite rumours to the contrary, Roy had never been pushed. It was purely his own decision to leave and go along a more rock'n'roll path than the more classical concept. Bill was not particularly happy with ELO or their prospects either, and he had been thinking of leaving anyway, when Roy told him he had an idea for a new band entirely and would like him to be part of it. Bill had always liked Roy's sense of humour and admired his musical talent, and was happy to go into the new band with him.

Hugh had a similar tale to tell. He thought Roy was being elbowed out by Jeff and the management and was feeling frustrated, especially in the recording studio. The main area of conflict seemed to be production, and Roy wanting more say in the process of what was to be committed to vinyl. Well aware that his long-term future in the band looked increasingly untenable, during the Italian tour he asked Bill and Hugh in confidence if they would be interested in a completely new project. Hugh's sympathies were with Roy, who was 'such a nice, friendly guy, and also very shy'.

Jeff and Bev had been none too happy with Roy's unexpected departure, as he had evidently kept his feelings to himself about the deteriorating situation. Roy believed that the only one who fully understood the situation from his point of view was Richard Tandy. Needless to say, the music press scented a major story, and all sides handled the matter with great discretion. As far as readers of the music weeklies were concerned, it was largely a matter of musical differences which could not accommodate both within the same band. Not until many years later did the full story emerge.

Wizzard's early days looked as though they would be dogged with the same confusion as those of ELO. Almost at once came the offer of 'an amazing gig' for their live debut, pencilled in for the bill on the all-star Rock'n'Roll gig at Wembley on 5 August. This was to be headed by Bill Haley and his Comets, Chuck Berry, Jerry Lee Lewis, Little Richard, Bo Diddley and others. Initial advance publicity billed them as The Move, and only altered it when Roy's management threatened legal action.

Not even their best friends could pretend that Wembley was a shattering debut. The teds took exception to their long hair and vivid costumes – shouts of 'Get off, you bloody fairies' greeted them as they walked onstage. The sound system did them no good either. Roy and Rick later explained that the p.a. was bad for everybody that day, and as far as Wizzard were concerned, they had to use whatever was available. The system they were provided with only had 15 of the 20 mikes necessary, and the mixing was lousy. Roy's amp blew up twice, and for the first time in his life onstage he took his guitar off and just sang. The sax players had only joined the band two days before, and were reading off music sheets on the floor; when the wind started blowing them around, they had to jump in the air to play it. It was the perfect recipe for chaos. Sound problems, if not gusts of wind onstage, would plague them on stage throughout much their career. But in spite of everything it was 'nice to be thrown in at the deep end' to a moderately well-received set featuring a rearranged *The Girl Can't Help It*, alongside several originals.

Roy conceded that, in the early days at least, their sound could have been much better live. By any standards, the eight-piece instrumental line-up was a staggeringly ambitious one. Trying to make cellos and sax heard over two drum kits was not the easiest thing in the world, and as money was made mainly from album sales, not live performances, they could not afford a top-class sound man, and had to get whoever was with the p.a. company at the time. In the early days they had decided to buy rather than rent a forty-channel custom-built p.a. system. They struggled with it for about two weeks before they opened it up to find the inputs wired to the outputs, bypassing all the channel controls except the fader volume. From then on, they rented.

Later in August they appeared at the Reading Festival, a bill which also included Mungo Jerry, Status Quo, Rod Stewart and the Faces, Ten Years After, Genesis and coincidentally ELO, playing their first date with the new post-Roy line-up. Pete Erskine of *Disc and Music Echo* summed Wizzard up after their performance as 'a nice band', playing fairly basic rock'n'roll 'but with a degree of finesse and power that's unusual'. They had however had one major problem at Reading when they found that the piano they had been given to play was out of tune. While the rest of the band were tuning up prior to their set, Rick called out, 'Give us an A,' and Bill, feeling the piano was not much good for anything else, did so literally – by tearing the A key out and throwing it to him. When they started their set, Roy could barely sing the first two numbers properly as he was laughing so much.

That autumn they took part in the Harvest mobile tour with some of the label's other acts. In *New Musical Express*, Nick Kent's verdict on them live was that, while there was great potential in the concept and that the tour should bring them into shape, they had a lot of tightening up to do. Roy, he went on, had 'forsaken the melodic content of his songs for the band for a more brutal rocking sound which does not quite become him. Bad mixing made the sound intolerable at points and some of the band members' stage antics were embarrassing.' Don Arden also had harsh words for some of their gigs, commenting that Roy's solution to any problems was to turn the volume up to such a deafening degree that punters would be walking out and asking for their money back. Yet a little later Pete Frame, of *Rock Family Trees* fame, would remark more perceptively that if ELO were discipline then Wizzard were fun; their early gigs were 'bizarre displays of drunken lunacy during which musical finesse was dramatically absent'. To Roy, Wizzard was very much a fun band; 'after earlier traumas, I was determined to just go onstage and have a good time, and that rubbed off on the audience.'

Yet the first single proved well worth waiting for. Issued in the first week of November, *Ball Park Incident* was described by John Peel in his review for *Disc* as 'an eccentric piece of work' which sounded as though they were playing on the platform at Notting Hill Gate underground station while someone held a mic at the other end of the Holland Park tunnel. Aided by heavy TV and radio exposure, after entering the charts modestly at No. 46 it climbed steadily over the Christmas season, peaking at No. 6 in January 1973, thus giving Roy what was at the time the probably unique distinction of having played a major role on and produced or co-produced three British top ten singles by different bands in the space of six months. The B-side was an instrumental, *Carlsberg*

Special (Pianos Demolished Phone 021 373 4472), written by Bill Hunt, based on a Bach Prelude. This was the start of Roy's policy of letting other members of the band contribute B-sides, rather than write tracks for the LPs, which was his contractual responsibility. As the singles sold better, this gave them a generous share of composing royalties. The tune was used as the theme music to a BBC4 documentary on Savile Row, which brought the composer an unexpected fillip in further royalties many years on. Rumours would persist that at least some of the B-sides were actually written by Roy, who 'gave' the composing credits to individual members in turn, but Rick was adamant that all the music was written by the credited authors, with everybody pitching in on arrangements.

The addition of Bill's phone number to the title – surely the polar opposite of going ex-directory – had been the band's idea, not his. He was unaware they were going to do it until the record appeared, and needless to say it rarely stopped ringing. Callers were friendly and genuinely surprised they were speaking to a member of one of the country's most successful bands, but as with all jokes, it wore thin after a while. The newly-married Mr and Mrs Hunt were eventually forced to change the number, and it was inadvertently reallocated to a lady in her eighties who was likewise continually pestered by people who had bought the single. She undoubtedly had no intention of moonlighting as a demolisher of pianos, and presumably also applied for a change of number.

As the press conference in July 1972 had stipulated, The Move's recording contract with EMI technically still had another two years to run. But as Wizzard and ELO had begun their recording careers with a Top 10 single each (*10538 Overture* had reached No. 9 during the summer), EMI allowed it to lapse, thus allowing Roy and Jeff to concentrate properly on what were evidently going to be two very successful new bands. There would be no more new Move singles or albums.

Elated by the unexpected success of *Ball Park*, Roy declared that Wizzard would issue far more singles than The Move ever did, and become 'a very strong singles band'. He defined them as 'basically a rock'n'roll band with jazz feelings', but admitted that audiences who came along to hear a whole set of material in the *Ball Park* vein might be disappointed. Above all, Roy said, he had 'never worked in a band with a greater good time feeling'. On their days off, he and the members of Wizzard sometimes went out together for a drink. That had never happened with the other groups, split by rivalry at best and thinly-veiled hostility at worst.

Recorded with the initial working title of 'We're Off To See The Wizzard', the LP 'Wizzard Brew' was released in March 1973. It managed to be clever, self-parodying, humorous, indulgent, cacophonous and pretty well everything else all at once. Echoing the unwritten rule of those days that LPs deliberately excluded tracks issued as singles, and were made up by and large of very long cuts, it boasted only three per side. These varied in length from the two-minute military march *Jolly Cup Of Tea*, to the 13½-minute *Meet Me At the Jailhouse*, a jam incorporating sax solos bouncing from one stereo channel to the other and heavy rock riffs on each other instrument. The live version of this often ran to a good 45 minutes. Two track were the right length and degree of commerciality to be potential 45s if necessary - *You Can Dance The Rock'n'Roll*, with screaming vocal compared by reviewers to that of Slade's Noddy Holder, then the hottest group around, and *Gotta Crush (About You)*, a clever doo-wop recreation. The segued *Buffalo Station-Get On Down To Memphis* was an inventive combination of almost everything, running the whole gamut from contemporary hard rock to a snatch of Elvis impersonation and even a short detour down Dixieland jazz band territory, and the 9-minute closing number *Wear A Fast Gun* was a tastefully epic ballad with French horn, flutes and a choral reprise of *Abide With Me*.

In retrospect, its everything but the kitchen sink sound and production meant there was too much to take in at once. The internet *All Music Guide* would later call it 'easily the noisiest damn record of its era – compressed, processed, and flattened within an inch of its life.'

To use a cliché, its strengths only appeared on repeated listens. Some critics, especially those who had heard a preview of the album in its early stages with a different running order, were better prepared for what to expect. When *Sounds* interviewer Mike Putland commented on the atmosphere and the dense sound, Roy conceded that it was easy to accuse them of sounding messy, as there was so much going on. But if people listened to it a few times, particularly with headphones, 'they'll really get into what the individual instruments are playing'. It is a verdict with which many fans would agree. The sheer complexity of the sound and the amount of what was going on meant that only on repeated listening over a long period of time was it possible to appreciate the artistry, attention to detail and even the sense of humour in an astonishingly diverse twelve inches of vinyl. What could easily be criticised as self-indulgence at first was soon revealed as a work of painstaking craftsmanship.

Yet it sold moderately, peaking in the charts at No. 29 during a seven-week run. It was probably a bit too experimental, Roy commented some years later, saying that he thought EMI wanted them in the studio to soon when they would have benefited with more time on stage. Perhaps there was something to be learnt from the fact that most of the other main glam rock acts, such as Slade, T. Rex and Gary Glitter, issued albums consisting of short tracks, nearly all potential singles, and would top the album chart or at least come very close. Sweet likewise recorded a long player, *Sweet Fanny Adams,* aimed at the album market, consisting mostly of fairly long tracks rather than possible hits, and it too only made the lower end of the Top 30 on release in spring 1974.

The present author remembers paying the grand sum of 90p for a ticket to see Wizzard on tour at Plymouth Guildhall in July 1973, in the days when the album would have cost about £2.25 brand new over the high street counter. Before they played *Buffalo Station/Get On Down To Memphis*, Rick announced, 'We're going to do a number from the 'Wizzard Brew' album next.' Somebody near the front of the crowd cheered, as Rick pointed in his direction and laughed, 'Great – the only bloke in the audience who's bought it!'

Bill Hunt thought that it 'missed its target with the public'. Like so many others, he saw Roy's greatest talent as a writer of pop singles, in that sense far more than Jeff Lynne, whose approach at the time was more suited to concept album tracks. Yet bands like Led Zeppelin and Pink Floyd had helped to make the album scene more important, a scene which did not suit Roy so well. 'Wizzard Brew' was so different from the singles, he thought, that 'the fans must have been flabbergasted!' If the singles were like the Spector sound, said one critic, the album was closer to the Don Ellis Orchestra. Nevertheless, he said that Roy was 'brilliant' to work with in the studio. He knew exactly what he wanted, he had the sound and concept in his head, and it was just a matter of working with the band to bring that sound out. Even so, everybody involved had their own ideas, which were always actively encouraged.

Though the long player may have baffled those who only knew Roy as a creator of concise hit singles, *See My Baby Jive,* a five-minute extravaganza with a nifty intro which segued the sounds of a revving motorbike into a thunderous drum sound and an exhilarating whoop that heralded the main melody line, and backing vocals by the Suedettes (Roy, Rick and Ayshea Brough, presenter of TV's *Lift Off*) was ample compensation. Released at the beginning of April, EMI Records eagerly promoted it in music press ads in the weekly music papers as 'the sound Phil Spector was aiming for', something which was done without the band's approval and rather irritated them.

Nevertheless, when they were mixing it they knew it would be a success, and it gave Roy his biggest hit to date. It entered the charts at No. 27, and climbed steadily. While it was doing so, Roy and Rick told Rob Mackie in *Sounds* that they were not sure about its chances as a chart-topper, as Sweet probably had the best chance with *Hellraiser* (which entered at No. 4 but stalled two places higher), but conceded it would be 'just nice to get up there in the top half'. In fact they managed it, for in May it leapfrogged *Hellraiser*, reached No. 1 and stayed there for four weeks. It ultimately became the sixth best-selling 45 in Britain that year – and in the Top 100 selling singles of the decade, the 100th.

The B-side, *Bend Over Beethoven*, credited to Hugh as a composer, was a gentle dig at the expense of ELO, who had just charted with their second single *Roll Over Beethoven.* Jeff was 'a bit choked about it,' said Roy, but 'we only did it for a laugh, not to knock them.' Even more cheekily, the label bore ('The official follow-up to 'California Man'!') after the composer credit. That had been added in a lighthearted moment by Roy, remembering that EMI's ads in the music press for ELO's *Roll Over Beethoven* had made a similar claim.

Beethoven had been the single, edited down by a couple of minutes, from ELO's second album, on part of which an uncredited Roy can be heard on bass. Although Roy had moved on from ELO, he still left a few small imprints on the band. He had played on *Queen of the Hours*, the B-side of *Beethoven*, an edit from the full-length version taken from the debut album. In addition he played bass on some tracks on 'ELO 2', released in March 1973, sessions for which had begun about a year earlier, although his contributions were not credited on the sleeve. Ironically, although he had left The Move partly to facilitate the formation of ELO, Carl did three tracks with the band at about this time in the studio, and they eventually found release as bonus cuts on the thirtieth anniversary double CD. Finally, original pressings on the label of ELO's third album, 'On The Third Day', released at the end of 1973, credited the music publishing to Roy Wood Music/Carlin/Music/Sugartown Music. Roy's name was removed on subsequent pressings. Rumours persisted, yet were denied, that he had played on the album itself.

At around the same time Bill Hunt left Wizzard, partly as his wife was expecting their first child, and because he preferred the security of a job in teaching music. He could see Roy being promoted more as a solo artist, and talking about gigs at the Albert Hall using different musicians like Rick Wakeman on keyboards. To him, there seemed to be no long-term future in the band. He was replaced by Bob Brady, another ex-Mongrel member, and long before that one of the Applejacks. Bill's nephew Miles Hunt would be leader of indie band the Wonder Stuff several years later, and Bill and Roy were invited to a do at the Townhouse Studio in London to celebrate the completion of one of their albums. Singer Kirsty MacColl was there with her husband, producer Steve Lillywhite, who had been a tape operator at the Marble Arch Studio where The Move, ELO and Wizzard had done much of their recording. Miles introduced Roy and Kirsty, who told him that at one time *See My Baby Jive* had been her favourite single.

By now Roy's visual image, with a warpainted star on his face, multicoloured robe and hairpieces, and tartan trousers, had become as instantly recognisable as those of contemporary glam-rockers like Bowie, Bolan and Sweet. Though there was criticism from some Move fans who thought he had sold out to the teenybop market, no *Top Of The Pops* was complete without the sight of Wizzard creating a party atmosphere in the studio to the sound of their current hit, amidst a merry mayhem of custard pies and pantomime horses, with roadies like Pete Shepherd and Richard Battle, or friends like Mike Sheridan, in gorilla costumes. More serious critics and readers of the music weeklies might write that Roy was demeaning his talent as a musician and performer with these childish antics on TV, but there was little doubt that the group helped to brighten up the music scene no end.

'Wizzard was very chaotic,' he admitted. 'We were thumbing our noses at bands who stood onstage doing nothing, just playing for themselves. We used to do the maddest things possible. People in the band cowered in dressing room corners, wondering what I would get them to do. Once Rick had an entire's angel costume to wear with roller skates.' Even so, they had several ideas rejected by *Top Of The Pops*, 'and there were a lot of things going on you never saw on screen, because the camera would focus elsewhere and miss a juggling or trampoline act. The original idea was for a rock'n'roll circus. I always wanted to organise the first rock pantomime, with us taking part in a plot, but we couldn't find anyone who was interested. It's the old story that if your records are doing all right, the record company doesn't feel the need to do anything different.'

Despite all the high jinks, *Top Of The Pops* had its down side for at least some of the band. Like everybody else they had to mime to the records, as groups inevitably did in those days unless they could sing live in the studio to a backing track, and it could be very tedious for them if they all had to hang around the BBC Shepherds Bush studios much of the day under the lights, doing nothing but just waiting for their turn to rehearse with the cameramen and lighting technicians. While they were filming a Christmas special for the show on one occasion, a very thirsty Mike and Nick decided they had had enough of this, so they slipped out, put on old greatcoats over their stage clothes and nipped out to the nearest off-licence where they bought a bottle of cider and went to sit on Shepherds Bush Green as they refreshed themselves. Almost at once a policeman came up to them and asked what they thought they were up to. Only then did they realise that they had inadvertently chosen a favourite spot for down-and-outs, all knocking back bottles of alcohol in brown paper bags. Fearful of being arrested for vagrancy, the musicians had to persuade the long arm of the law that they were in fact two members of one of the country's most successful groups, about to go on the nation's top pop show and doing no more than taking a brief break in their work. While it might have made for interesting publicity, to arrest them might be more than a little embarrassing for all concerned.

The band had its own fan club, Wizzard Watchas' Society, run by Mike Sheridan. Part of his brief was to write letters to the fans who wrote in, post off the T-shirts – and also look after Roy's Old English sheepdog, which stank and 'wrecked the house...camel breath'. Another little job he undertook from time to time was to appear on TV dressed, masked and bewigged as a second Roy Wood, to join in the miming.

Suddenly everyone wanted Roy to produce their records. Ian Hunter, front man of Mott The Hoople, particularly liked the horn section in Wizzard and was so impressed with *See My Baby Jive* that he tried to obtain his services as the producer of their 1973 album 'Mott', following the end of their connection with David Bowie who had helped to put them back on their feet in 1972 when they had more or less decided to split, and launched them as a household name at last by writing and producing their top three hit *All The Young Dudes*. Their first hit of 1973, *Honaloochie Boogie*, used cello and saxophone in a manner unashamedly reminiscent of Roy's style, and further similarities would be evident in a subsequent hit *The Golden Age Of Rock'n'Roll* a year later. However his idolisation of Roy was not unanimously shared by the band, with bassist Overend Watts thinking the records sounded messy. But as Roy's time was severely limited, Hunter did the next best thing by hiring engineer Bill Price, who had been working with Wizzard, to help out on the album which the band produced themselves. American acts such as Paul Butterfield, Tony Joe White and Earthquake also asked Roy at around this time but in vain to take the producer's seat for their new recordings.

Another was Sparks, led by American brothers Ron and Russell Mael, who in the 21st century would still place a 'Best Of The Move' compilation in their list of top five all-time favourite albums. On an early visit to England in late 1972 Sparks had opened for ELO, shortly after Roy's departure, at the University of East Anglia. Good as ELO were, they had always recognised Roy as the essence of The Move, and were convinced that if asked to put their proverbial shirt on either new band, Wizzard was the one which would get their vote as far more likely to make it. When they came to record their breakthrough album 'Kimono My House' in London, Roy was their first choice as producer, but once again he was unavailable at the time.

Yet another major artist of the time who commented approvingly on both bands was Bryan Ferry. He was interviewed by Roy Hollingworth of *Melody Maker* at around the time the second Roxy Music album, 'For Your Pleasure', was released, as they were sitting in a pub where the jukebox was playing *Roll Over Beethoven*. Ferry said he loved Jeff Lynne's voice, but Roy Wood's was better. 'When I was a DJ I had a habit of playing *Fire Brigade* every night.' It also emerged that the young Freddie Mercury was an ardent admirer of Roy Wood, particularly The Move albums.

One performer who did manage to receive Roy's attention in the studio during his limited time available was Ayshea Brough, with whom he was romantically involved for a while. He wrote, played all instruments on and produced her single *Farewell*, released under the name of Ayshea on a one-off deal with Harvest at the end of April 1973. In view of his high profile at the time, it was perhaps surprising that the record was completely ignored by Radio 1, although some listeners had a theory that it was in effect off-limits because she was a TV presenter 'on the other side', namely ITV. Despite some airplay on Radio Luxembourg, it failed to chart. If Roy had had his way, he said, he would have probably spent more time in the studio with others, and correspondingly less on the road, but the rest of Wizzard, he explained apologetically, had to eat. He was lucky to grab four hours sleep a night anyway with his hectic schedule.

The success of Wizzard gave Roy the chance to fulfil another long-shelved ambition, release of his solo LP 'Boulders'. Begun in the studio during his spare time some three or four years earlier while The Move were still enjoying success, and completed early in January 1972, it added new meaning to the hackneyed term 'solo album', which all too often meant members of established bands putting out indifferent sets recorded with other musicians more for self-satisfaction than for anything else. Roy wrote, played each instrument apart from harmonium on the first track, played by EMI studio engineer John Kurlander, sang every vocal on and produced 'Boulders', and also painted the front sleeve design.

The first single from it had surfaced in January 1972, *When Gran'ma Plays The Banjo*, a novelty number put out on 45, he said, because his Mum liked it, on which he sounded like a dead ringer for John Fogerty. Once again it had been totally ignored by Radio 1, and never stood a chance of making the charts, although it did receive exposure one week on ITV's *Lift Off*. Another track, *Songs Of Praise*, the one featuring harmonium, had been recorded by the New Seekers and shortlisted for the Eurovision Song Contest in 1972. Some of the other songs allowed Roy to indulge his love of rock'n'roll, particularly *Rock Down Low* (which was preceded by a brief snatch of the vocal backing to *Dear Elaine* backwards with his voice at various speeds) and *Locomotive*, both of which had partly inspired the basic Wizzard sound, and both of which were included in the band's live set for a while. Others had a more folksy feel with one, *All The Way Over The Hill*, ending up as a jig, *The Irish Loafer (And His Hen)*. *Wake Up* featured probably the most eccentric percussion track of all, nothing less than stereo water splashes in a bucket performed faithfully by Roy, who was clad on the suggestion of engineer Alan Parsons in a yellow sou'wester as he did so.

His own favourite track, *Miss Clarke And The Computer*, was perhaps the strangest, most experimental track of the whole lot. A wry story song with a computer (in an era long before personal computers, laptops and notebooks had entered everyday life) having human feelings and falling in love with the engineer who came to repair it, the instrumentation included electric sitar, cello, string bass, acoustic nylon guitars and Welsh harp – with a jazzy break in the middle. Premiered on stage during the early days of ELO, *Dear Elaine*, a haunting Tudor ballad backed mainly by lute, cello and recorder, was chosen as the new single. It was released in August, and peaked at No. 18 the following month. It had originally been scheduled for issue the previous October and allocated a catalogue number but then pulled from the schedule, presumably as all EMI's promotional resources were then focused on Wizzard and the imminent first single.

One of the engineers at Abbey Road who helped to work on the album was Alan Parsons, who would go on to produce albums for such artists as Al Stewart, John Miles, and his own Alan Parsons Project, as well as score consecutive chart-topping singles early in 1975 with Pilot and Steve Harley & Cockney Rebel. He was partly responsible for some of the novel sounds to be heard on 'Boulders', such as the two tambourines Roy was using at once and hitting against a filing cabinet on the off-beat on *Songs Of Praise*, and making the voice get lower and lower on *Miss Clarke And The*

Computer, as the lyrics of the song told of the computer's screws being undone. From Roy, Alan learnt several tricks of the trade such as using a slightly faster or slower pitch each time when double-tracking. It was a technique that he would frequently use on his own productions.

Although 'Boulders' had been ready to release around the time of 'Message From The Country', management and other members of The Move maintained that the latter band was more important, and to issue it would be a distraction that would cost The Move dearly in terms of record sales. However, where 'Message' had soldmodestly and failed to make any impact on the charts whatsoever, the outstanding 'Boulders' outsold all his group albums, peaking at No. 15 in September during an eight-week run. Even so, by this time it seemed like an old record to Roy, who had long since moved on to other things.

While both single and album were shifting well, they were overtaken by Wizzard's third single *Angel Fingers*, credited on the label as 'a teen ballad, with vocal backing by the Suedettes and the Bleach Boys'. The song's introduction was as carefully crafted as ever. Roy wanted the sound of a tubular bell (Mike Oldfield influences, anyone?) in the intro, going up in pitch, 'so I whacked it, and as I hit it we slowed the tape down, so that then when we played the tape back it would be speeded up so the bell would go [makes noise] – but it didn't. Well, at least my science class wasn't that wasted. I got a bucket of water and took the bell off its stand, hit the bell, dunked it in the water, and it went donggggg – perfect!'

Angel Fingers proved to be Roy's fastest selling single yet, entering in its first week at No. 12 and giving Wizzard a second No. 1, albeit only staying there for one week. Coincidentally it bested Sweet for a second time, with their rivals mortified to see *Ballroom Blitz* entering at No. 2 and blocked from rising any further, firstly by *Angel Fingers* for one week and then by the Simon Park Orchestra's middle-of-the-road instrumental *Eye Level*, the theme from TV's *Van Der Valk* drama series, for a further two. The B-side, a song written by Rick Price, *You Got The Jump On Me*, was a remarkably un-Wizzard-like piece, with Robert Plant-like vocals and no brass or woodwind within sight or sound. If you sprung it on your unsuspecting friends and stopped them from seeing that it was a 45 on the Harvest label, they would probably ask why they had never heard that Led Zeppelin number before. Rick did not sing on it as, in his words, Roy transposed it 'into a key which only a dog can hear'.

With this unexpected level of success came the necessity of broadening Wizzard's stage act on tour. They had to compromise on the jazz-rock intentions and put on more of a pop show, especially for ABC Theatre dates. It was not just the student audience, but also mums and dads bringing their kids along.

Another extra-curricular venture came about when Roy was invited to play bass, while Keith Smart and Charlie Grima, played drums on three tracks recorded by Bo Diddley in London. A little misleadingly, the album also included six cuts recorded in Chicago with different musicians. Despite this, the set was released under the title 'The Bo Diddley London Sessions'.

Shortly before *Angel Fingers*, Hugh left the band and they were down to a seven-piece. The decision, he said, had been mainly down to Roy, who was taking them more in a big band direction. Bandless for a short spell, he did some cello teaching, until the wheel came full circle. One of ELO's cellists, Colin Walker, had just married and announced his intention to leave, so Hugh rejoined the band and remained for several years.

Although it was not the most successful Wizzard single in chart position terms, peaking at No. 4, the record which would stamp their name into the rock history books more than any other was *I Wish It Could Be Christmas Everyday*. Mike Burney would later claim at least partial responsibility for the inspiration; 'I'd been doing really boring big band gigs on the ballroom circuit, so when Roy offered me a job in Wizzard I was just knocked out. I used to say to him, "Roy, being in this band, it's like Christmas every day." And, as far as I know, Roy picked up on that as a song title.'

The track was initially recorded during a blazing hot summer, about four months previously. Steve Brown, the tape operator, recalled that during the early stages when the rest of the band went out for a curry and Roy stayed behind, they removed all the lights and replaced them with blue bulbs to make the place look colder and create the right ambience. Roy sent the roadies out to go and fetch some fans (not girls, but the cooling kind with motors which plug in), and decorate the place with tinsel, silver balls and fairy lights around the speakers. By the time the band returned in, the studio was indeed a winter wonderland, and it was so cold that everyone had to wrap up suitably dressed in coats, bobble hats and scarves to help create the right atmosphere.

The whole magnum opus was as carefully constructed as the previous Wizzard records. Roy started by putting a click track down, just a cow bell, on quarter-inch tape, then played the arrangement on acoustic guitars and double-tracked it. 'It wasn't a demo, as such, because it became the basis for the whole song. We just overdubbed everything else on top.' It started with a clever joke, or perhaps a wry comment on the over-commercialisation of the festive season, depending on one's point of view – the sound of a cash register. 'We got a sound effects record but it was crap, so we hired a proper old fashioned metal cash register with all the scroll work on the sides, and I pressed the buttons while Rick dropped the coins in. It was exactly what I wanted.'

No effort was spared. Bill said that Roy was 'amazing about drums. He hired loads of unusual percussion instruments, shakers and scrapers and maracas, then he threw them all into a big bass drum case and shook the case to see what it sounded like. And, sure enough, it sounded like nothing you'd ever heard before.' Keith Smart also recalled that on the first day of working on the single, 'we recorded until 8 a.m. the next morning just to get the drum sounds he wanted. Rather than close-mike everything in a booth, he used ambience mikes to get a big Phil Spectorish sound. When we went back into the studio the next day and listened, he didn't like it any more. Some tiny detail wasn't right, so we dumped those tapes and did another 12-hour session to get it right.'

Equal care was given to getting the vocals right, according to Rick. 'We always tried to get a sort of party vibe when we recorded the vocals. I would do a lot of the high and low vocal parts. We didn't go in for drugs, but mostly we were drunk. I can still smell every breath of vodka in that record.'

Added to the mythical Suedettes on backing vocals were children's voices, a label credit reading 'with additional noises by Miss Snob and Class 3C'. The twelve-strong Stockland Green School 1st Year Choir were chosen for the honour as the school's maths teacher was the brother-in-law of Bill Hunt. Roy was very keen to have a children's choir, said Bill, 'and he insisted it had to be Birmingham kids, even though we were recording in London, so I got the job of sorting it out. I lived near Stockland Green School in

Slade Road, which always amused me because in the end we battled it out with Slade for the No 1 spot.'

After being selected through a rather embarrassing audition at school assembly, singing hymns unaccompanied, they rehearsed their parts there on 29 October during half-term and travelled to London next day to add their voices to the recording.

'We came down in a coach, and we got loads of pop and crisps in the back for the kids, a crate of Newcastle Brown for the band,' Roy explained. 'It was a school project for them – they had to write what it was like to be in a recording studio and as we got there, to Phonogram at Marble Arch, I showed them the mixer desk, all the stuff, explained how a record was made, and they were writing all this stuff down on notepads. By the time they came to do the vocals they were really relaxed, and on the second take they did it perfectly.' The only disappointing part for the children was that they had expected the whole band to be there, but it was just Mr Wood – without his stage or TV make-up on - and a pair of headphones. To compensate for this, when they asked him if his hair was real, he allowed them to pull it. They recorded their contribution several times, with each part being built up on tape to make it sound like a really large choir. When it was done, they sat on the sofa listening to it, as Roy shouted, 'What number will we get to?' – and they all screamed back, 'Number one!'

Afterwards they were taken to the Hard Rock Cafe nearby in Roy's Rolls-Royce where tables had been booked, with one member of the band at each table while the youngsters were treated to burgers and banana splits. They were not paid, one of them recalled, 'but when it was all over, [Roy] gave us each a Wizzard album, and as many badges as we could carry. Mine said, "I'm busting for a Wizz." I was terrified of what my mother would say when she saw it. He promised us all a copy of the single, but I'm still waiting!'

Roy was thrilled at the children's contribution to the song. 'When I was in the control room listening to the kids singing what I'd written, I got really choked up, and the hairs were standing up on the back of my neck.'

In 2005, under the terms of new copyright legislation, it was ruled that the children, each of whom had been traced and were now in their early forties, would receive royalty payments of several hundred pounds each for their contributions to the record.

At the time, yuletide singles by established pop and rock acts had been few and far between, with the exception of John Lennon and Yoko Ono's *Happy Christmas (War Is Over)*, a top five hit in Britain the previous year. From 1963 to 1965, and again in 1967, the Christmas No. 1 was always the Beatles' latest, after which the festive No. 1 then by tradition tended to be a novelty song by some all-round entertainer or name whose chances of charting with such a song at any other time of the year were minimal. In 1968 it had been the turn of the Scaffold *(Lily The Pink)*, followed next year by Rolf Harris (*Two Little Boys*), then next - or technically speaking in the first post-Christmas chart - *Dad's Army* actor Clive Dunn (*Grandad*), and then by Benny Hill (*Ernie (The Fastest Milkman In The West)*). By now it was time for a change, and Roy was keen to make a festive single because the idea had been unfashionable for years. 'We thought it would be worth trying a real rock'n'roll Christmas song.'

Little did Wizzard know that at about the same time Slade were in a sweltering hot studio while touring on the other side of the Atlantic, likewise putting *Merry Xmas Everybody* on tape, with bassist Jim Lea playing John Lennon's harmonium on the track. Elton John likewise chipped in that same season with *Step Into Christmas*, although it stalled well short of the Top 20. Slade could at that time hardly do anything wrong chartwise in Britain, and their festive song became the third Slade single to fly straight into the chart at pole position that year. Bill Hunt fondly remembered how Wizzard got their own back for being pipped at the post (though admittedly previous and future chart-topping singles by Gary Glitter and The New Seekers were also helping to make the top three a no-go area for anyone else in those vital yuletide weeks). When both Midlands bands were on *Top Of The Pops*, a staged custard pie fight took place. 'While Slade were on, one of our drummers sneaked into the audience and hit Noddy full in the face with one. If you see the video, you'll notice that Noddy doesn't appear again after that.' Naturally there were no hard feelings as all members joined each other in the bar afterwards.

There was however one problem with the programme in which Roy had no say. 'For *Top Of The Pops*, I really wanted to use the school kids but we had to use Equity children, so we got them from the Italia Conti acting school. I was really brassed off because the kids they sent were much too big, and they didn't even know the song, so half of them just stood there. They didn't even sing the words.'

By now Roy was signed simultaneously to two different record companies. The deal with EMI/Harvest still stood for his work as a solo artist, the natural successor to The Move deal, but the next few Wizzard releases were to appear on the Warner Bros label. Such was the confusion that Warners originally released *I Wish It Could Be Christmas Everyday*.

'There was some funny business going on,' said Roy, 'because we were contracted to Harvest, but Don Arden did a deal for the single with Warner Brothers. They even got as far as pressing them up before EMI found out and came storming in and demanded it be on Harvest. Don operated in his own unique ways. You could never figure out what was going on in his mind.' Initial copies therefore appeared in a vividly-decorated gatefold sleeve and most of these were bought up by EMI, who stuck the Harvest logo and number over the Warner Bros info. Despite this, a plentiful number of Warner copies escaped on to the collectors' market.

When Roy was asked some years later which was his favourite Wizzard single, this was his choice, 'because I felt like I had succeeded in bringing a Disney image into sound.' On another occasion, he commented, 'People talk about it being over-produced, but the effect I was trying to get was something I personally associate with Christmas, that Walt Disney music feel. It's Disney movie music without the film.'

The B-side, *Rob Roy's Nightmare (A Bit More H.A.)*, was an instrumental by Mike Burney. It peaked at No. 4 at the height of the Yuletide season (Slade scooping the honours at No. 1), four rungs higher than Roy's second solo hit *Forever* which would peak at No. 8 in January, giving him his only Top 10 hit as a soloist.

Forever was described by him as an affectionate act of homage to the Beach Boys and Neil Sedaka. Like many a fan, he had thought how great it would be if both appeared on one record. Such a possibility being remote to say the least, he went into the studio intending to emulate the way such a union would sound. Carl Wilson quickly voiced his approval, while Neil Sedaka sent Roy a telegram to say: 'Thrilled and flattered by your mention of my name. A devoted fan.'

1973 had been a remarkable year for Roy. Wizzard's first four singles had all gone Top 10 (two at No. 1, a feat only surpassed those twelve months by Slade with three), and another solo single was hovering on the brink, while the other had gone Top 20, thus giving him an aggregate of 52 chart weeks. Towards the end of the year he was invited to take part in Lou Reizner's charity presentation of Pete Townshend's 'Tommy' at the Rainbow Theatre, London, on 14 and 15 December. For Great Britain it was a grim time, with the advent of the three-day week, and television closing down at 10.30 p.m. every night in order to conserve power. But for Roy Wood, things had rarely if ever looked better from a professional point of view.

Such success, obviously, could not be sustained indefinitely. The stress and strain of touring, writing, producing and recording to fulfil two simultaneous contracts led to a stomach ulcer. Early in 1974 Roy arranged a party for the parents of each member of Wizzard. They were to see the gig and have a celebration afterwards. As always the perfectionist, he spent the day rehearsing and double-checking to make sure everything would go smoothly. Afterwards he collapsed, and for the next few months he was under doctor's orders to take it more gently.

The most immediate casualty was Wizzard's live work. The 2 March 1974 issue of *New Musical Express* carried a cover feature and interview with Roy, as well as letters from two disgruntled readers who had been to the band's gig, with Raymond Froggatt as support, at Ipswich Gaumont on 10 February. The show was short, extremely loud, distorted, and in the words of one of them, 'the most deplorable that I have ever been subjected to'. When he was granted a right of reply by the editor, Roy explained that the ulcer trouble had already been suspected, he had a dodgy throat, and two houses to get through that night. After performing he had gone straight back to bed to recover.

The first official releases for Warner Bros were postponed, as were several tour dates. The single *Rock'n'Roll Winter (Looney's Tune)*, recorded and released in mono, did not reach the shops until an unseasonally fine and sunny April, hence an apology on the label, 'Sorry the word Spring wouldn't fit. R.W.' 'Looney' was the band's nickname for Lynsey de Paul, with whom Roy was a good friend (or more) at the time. Like the two previous Wizzard singles, it reached the Top 10 in its second week, rising to a peak of No. 6.

It was soon followed by another solo hit (No. 13), and Roy's last new release on Harvest. *Goin' Down The Road (A Scottish Reggae Song)* featured assorted farmyard noises, two-tone car horn, mandolins and multi-tracked bagpipes. Using the last instrument on the record had caused some problems. Roy had only put down part of the bagpipe section in the studio when he ran out of breath, and an engineer was asked to supply the wind while Roy fingered the pipes. It was hard work, and both of them collapsed in a heap afterwards. As John Lennon once remarked, genius is pain. Its chart run coincided with *Top Of The Pops* being off the air for several weeks owing to a Musicians' Union strike (with re-runs of the World War II-based sitcom *Dad's Army* filling the vacant slot, on the grounds that according to BBC executives both programmes had the same audiences), thus denying Roy an invaluable promotion window and almost certainly preventing the single from reaching the Top 10.

When not on the road or watching his health, Roy was working simultaneously on three new LPs – a second solo set, 'Mustard', a more experimental double album (perhaps it should have been four new LPs, then); and a set of early rock'n'roll pastiches, the two latter projects with Wizzard. Some of the out-takes from this period which were never destined to see release included the instrumentals *Lungburger* (in two parts) and *The Lark*, both of which in their classical approach were closer to Roy's work on the first ELO album, a Tudor-style drinking song *Gentlemen*, an eleven-minute comic jazz spoof, *Mike Burney In Concrete* (at Ronnie Botts – or for the uninitiated, 'Mike Burney In Concert At Ronnie Scott's'); and their own version of B. Bumble & the Stingers' *Nut Rocker*, a rock'n'roll instrumental based on part of Tchaikovsky's *Nutcracker*, which had topped the British charts in 1962 and returned to the Top 20 as a reissue in the summer of 1972.

The last of these projects, 'Introducing Eddy And The Falcons', was the first to appear in the shops. It was 'originally going to be a double album, with each side in a different style, because there were so many things the band could play. I thought we could do one side rock'n'roll, one side classical, another side jazz, and the fourth a Rick price country-rock thing. We did the rock'n'roll side first, and Warners got a little impatient, so we ended up just releasing that.'

Packaged in a gatefold sleeve with a full-length colour poster of Roy in all his stage regalia, it was issued to excellent reviews in the first week of August 1974. Although all the songs were credited as a composer to Roy, he had been under pressure to complete them in a hurry, and Dick Plant, who 'was very good with words', helped out with some of the lyrics. Gene Vincent, Dion, Elvis Presley, Cliff Richard and others were all parodied with affection and good humour, in a collection of original songs which sounded almost like an album of greatest hits from the rock'n'roll era. *Come Back Karen* sounded almost more like Neil Sedaka than Sedaka himself. Rick had admitted that 'Wizzard Brew' was 'a bit outside the rules', but agreed that the second album was excellent. Side 1 even began Sergeant Pepper-style, to the sound of an audience going berserk as a compere breathlessly introduced the arrival of Eddy and the Falcons on stage. The introduction segued into *Eddy's Rock*, a guitar and sax instrumental which lovingly evoked Duane Eddy's 45s of a bygone era.

By an odd error of judgment, one of the less commercial tracks was chosen as the single. The ballad *This Is The Story Of My Love (Baby)* had never been intended as a 45, 'but when people began leaving Wizzard around that time because of management problems, they released it quick.' Without any promotion on TV, the record followed up five consecutive top tenners by struggling to a highest position of No. 34. Had reviewers had their way, the choice might have fallen on the more catchy *You Got Me Runnin'*, later covered by rock revival band Smiley & Co, getting some Radio 1 airplay if little sales, or the Del Shannon's *Runaway*-inspired *Everyday I Wonder*. According to the discography in Pete Frame's *Rock Family Trees*, *You Got Me Runnin'* was issued as a single in October 1974 with a previously-unavailable B-side, *It's Just My Imagination*. Various sources suggest that this entry was indeed just the author's imagination. But almost every track on the album could have been lifted off for general consumption on 7", as would probably have been the case if it had been released three or four years later. And there was some compensation for the band when the LP peaked at No. 19.

That autumn, Roy and Rick were invited to do a short promotional tour of radio stations around LA. A handful of tracks, including the pick of the hits and numbers from the two albums, and a saxes-led instrumental, *Salt Peanuts*, had been recorded at Shepperton Studios, Surrey, the previous year, with added crowd noises to make them sound like they had been taken from a live performance. These were circulated to various radio stations, and inevitably some found their way onto bootleg recordings over the years. The band were wined and dined by executives from Warner Bros, provided with chauffeurs, guides, tickets to Disneyland and to a Carole King concert. A meeting with Elvis was arranged, postponed and finally cancelled altogether, but a rendezvous with Brian Wilson was a different matter. They were taken to his house in a limousine and sat in his music room for half an hour before being invited into what looked like a garage with a bed in it. They were unprepared for the sight of a horrendously bloated Brian, very overweight and bedridden, lying on his back and barely able to turn his head to look at them. It was a pitiful occasion, and as they left Rick feared he had just seen a dead man. Nobody could have foreseen that Dennis Wilson would die in 1983, Carl in 1998, and that partly as a tribute to their memory Brian, who had by then recovered and was looking and sounding in remarkably good form, would go out on tour with a band playing the Beach Boys' 'Pet Sounds' album live in its entirety several years after that.

At around the same time, in September and October 1974, Wizzard undertook their long-awaited first American tour. They were eagerly awaited over there, as The Move had long been a cult band there despite (or maybe because of) never having had a major hit single but being the darlings of some of the more influential rock critics. The Move's first LP had never seen US release at the time, and to fill this gap A & M released a double compilation 'The Best of The Move', featuring the entire debut album, plus a handful of A- and B-sides from early singles, and sleeve notes by Bev Bevan. ELO were already building a following, partly due again to a belated Move fascination, and everyone wanted to see the group's other offshoot.

As for Wizzard themselves, they looked forward to their first US tour as something of a new start. Playing a more pop-oriented set to family audiences had become frustrating, and this could easily be discarded in favour of their jazz-rock inclinations in a country where audiences would not be calling out for their hits – as they had not had any there. 'Introducing Eddy' had been well-received on US release, and it was gratifying to hear people asking them to play tracks at gigs. Other highlights of their stage act included a nod to Move days in a more jazzy rearrangement of *California Man/Brontosaurus*, which inspired Illinois band Cheap Trick to record a more rock-oriented cover version four years later, a gentler acoustic song *She'll Be Home*, featuring the band on flutes and bells, *Goin' Down the Road*, with a lengthy bagpipe medley including tunes like *Scotland the Brave*, Bob Brady's song *Gang Bang*, featuring the writer himself on vocal as well as keyboards, and even a snatch of the classics courtesy of *Dance of the Toy Flutes*, from Tchaikovsky's *Nutcracker Suite*. Of all the dates they played in America, which took in New York, Los Angeles and Santa Monica, California, among other venues, the one at New Jersey, The Joint in the Woods, was for them the highlight – a packed, hot, sweaty venue attended by a very enthusiastic crowd.

Miraculously, Brian Wilson had made a speedy recovery, phoned Roy to say hello and invited them back to his house. It was totally unexpected and Roy almost fainted with surprise. When he and Rick went to the Wilson residence, Brian's daughters came to the gate, singing *Forever* in harmony (someone had had the forethought to send a copy of the single to the Wilsons in advance), which they proceeded to continue to do all the way up to the front door. Yet the meeting almost did not happen. Roy and Rick hung around for nearly an hour, talking to a woman from the record company as Brian was not around, and had to leave without seeing him. A couple of weeks later, having learnt that the Beach Boys were working with Brian on what would be released about eighteen months later as the '15 Big Ones' album, Roy received another call inviting them to the Brother Studio.

They had some interviews that day and went later than they had planned. When Roy, Mike and Nick arrived, the Beach Boys had just finished work and were coming out of the studio. Brian opened the car door and put on the tape for the backing track to one of the songs in progress, *It's OK*. Roy was knocked out, told them how much he liked it (as if one would dare say anything else on such an occasion), and they unlocked the studio so they could carry on working. The result was that the three members of Wizzard ended up playing drums and saxes and adding vocals on the track, which not only appeared on the album but was also a Top 30 single in the States. When Roy found himself standing at the microphone next to Carl and Brian Wilson as he sang with them, he thought he had died and gone to heaven - 'absolutely flippin' great!' Performing with two of the people he had so long admired above nearly all others in the music world was like a dream come true.

Perhaps it was no coincidence that Roy's next solo 45, *Oh What a Shame*, released in May 1975, also owed not a little to the Beach Boys in the vocal harmony department and, as some might have said bore a faint resemblance in the melody line to *Heroes And Villains*. Backed by an ingenious sitar-bagpipe instrumental *Bengal Jig*, and with initial copies sold in a self-drawn cartoon picture sleeve of Roy being pursued by a bass drum on legs, it peaked at No. 13 that summer. It turned out to be his last appearance in the British Top 20 for over thirty years.

Still Roy's head and imagination teemed with projects, many of which were never fulfilled. Plenty of material - presumably including *She'll Be Home* - was recorded at about this time but never issued. Roy mentioned in an interview that eight tracks put down at one studio were temporarily out of reach because of a dispute. Undaunted, he simply went to another studio and put down another seven there. It would not be surprising to learn that he probably dashed from that particular interview to load half a dozen instruments in the back of his car and drive to the next studio. Another scheme that sadly never came to fruition was for a solo concert at Christmas 1974 with Roy accompanied by the Royal Philharmonic Orchestra, due to be taped for a live LP. Whether Roy actually needed the musicians to play is open to doubt. In his case it might have been quicker to do the arrangements in his head, hire the instruments and get an engineer to overdub the applause, if an LP was the ultimate objective.

In other interviews at this stage Roy seemed at a loss to account for his inspiration as a songwriter. 'My songwriting anyway is mainly fictional, it always has been, so I don't have personal experiences to write about.' People who wrote songs to express their own feelings were 'really a bit boring'. The melodies always came more easily. Sometimes if he was inspired by a good title, as he had been on *I Can Hear the Grass Grow*, he would work on that. But more often it was a case of writing the tune first, recording a backing track in the studio, and then working on the words when he got home. Even if he had songs already written or in various embryonic stages, he would play a few old rock'n'roll tracks to get in the mood to complete the idea. The Beatles, collectively and individually, cropped up in conversation at regular intervals. For him, John Lennon's 'Imagine' was one of his favourite LPs, and the best thing any of them had done since the split. Though his work with Wings had yielded initially disappointing albums, Paul McCartney was still a genius - 'he'll never know how much he helped me with my writing.' In the light of Paul's collaborations with Stevie Wonder and Michael Jackson in the early 1980s, a McCartney-Wood joint effort would have been an interesting prospect to say the least. Led Zeppelin were for him the best rock band in the world, and Jimmy Page was the best rock guitarist.

At one time, it seemed as if the sky was the limit for Wizzard. There was even a rumour that they were going to star in their own situation comedy on TV. However, beyond a couple of executives – whom one likes to hope were fervent fans – presenting the idea to Don Arden, nothing further came of it. An album 'Bathe Your Feet', by Wizzard without Roy, basically featuring Rick on vocals, guitar and bass, Charlie on drums and Bob on keyboards, was also said to have been recorded, mainly as a result of Arden's wanting to keep them busy while Roy was engaged in other projects. Somewhere out there, therefore, lurks another album by the group, if the tapes can be located or if anyone owns up to having them.

While Wizzard were touring the US, Roy was flattered to hear that at least one of the former Beatles was an ardent admirer. Someone arrived with a cassette they had just recorded from the radio, featuring John Lennon talking about British rock. In it he had remarked that The Move were 'like the Hollies with balls', and paid Roy several compliments as a performer and musician. In particular he referred to the performance of *Brontosaurus* on TV, and had been so knocked out after seeing it that he phoned several of his friends, telling them they had to watch as well. When asked which were his favourite British songwriters, without hesitation he named Roy Wood and Jeff Lynne. 'It was great to hear Lennon's voice saying that,' remarked Roy. 'I'd love to get a copy of that show.'

Roy modestly never seemed to think of himself as a first division songwriter. Such was apparently not the view of Mick Farren, when reviewing 'The Roy Wood Story' compilation double LP in *New Musical Express*, on release in April 1976. According to him, Roy had been apparently in hot pursuit of Pete Townshend for the title of premier British post-Beatles/Stones songwriter for a long time, but Roy's 'complex little songs did not fit in with the current demands of public taste' during the late 1960s obsession with guitar heroes. The contest - such as it was - only ended when Pete wandered off to be Gilbert and Sullivan and Roy, 'using the established bopper media', tried turning 'crass pop into a weird art form'.

In December 1974 the band released *Are You Ready To Rock*, an ultra-commercial 45 and the follow-up to the comparatively unsuccessful *Story Of My Love*. This was good old basic 1950s rock'n'roll, much of it close to the sound pioneered twenty years before by Bill Haley and his Comets. Unusually it was only a little over two minutes long, half the length of the average Wizzard single, and even more unusually most of it was basically written over only three chords. Yet like so many of their other singles, in Roy's words it had 'a little something extra on the end for musos' – in this case, a coda on bagpipes, in a completely different key – as bagpipes are only in one key, which was a different one to the rest of the song. With generous radio and TV exposure it restored them to chart favour, reaching No. 8 in January 1975. But it would be their last Top 10 single, and little did anyone know that time was running out for them.

Although it may not have made them chart stars, Wizzard's first US tour had been a success on balance. The band had enjoyed playing to more open-minded audiences, and although it had not brought them any chart success there yet, their reception was very encouraging. It was not however a view shared by Don Arden, who feared that the Americans could not understand a word of his Brummie accent on stage, and tried to persuade him to take speech therapy.

Unfortunately the group's days were numbered. With initially eight, then seven, members, it was always going to be an expensive outfit to maintain. Roy was the ultimate perfectionist in the studio, and as such was undoubtedly an inspiration to others. Wizzard's singles had a certain amount in common with those of 10cc, being painstakingly constructed, multi-chorded epics yet still radio-friendly enough to make the upper echelons of the chart. Perhaps it was significant that when the Manchester quartet released their third album, 'The Original Soundtrack', in the spring of 1975, one track in particular attracted considerable attention and airplay despite its six-minute length. *I'm Not In Love* featured a massive amount of vocal overdubbing to produce the sound of a 256-voice choir, yet the record company still had reservations about its commercial appeal as a 45. Roy was one of those who urged the group to insist on it, and apparently sent a telegram to Eric Stewart, the member of 10cc primarily responsible for writing it, saying it was an obvious choice for a single if ever there was one. In slightly edited form, it proved Roy and others right, giving the band their second chart-topper that June.

Nevertheless Wizzard's recording costs were enormous, and business acumen was never one of Roy's strong points. According to Rick, when they finished *Angel Fingers*, it was rumoured that they had spent more time in the studio than Paul McCartney had done during sessions for the whole of Wings' 'Band On The Run' album. With most of the money paid by EMI being eaten up in bills for such purposes, the band members were relying heavily on live touring work for their income, and two tours of the UK plus one of the US did not provide them with regular wages.

In an interview with Bob Harris on *The Old Grey Whistle Test*, shown in April 1975, Roy mentioned that a second American tour was planned for Wizzard, scheduled to begin in July 1975 and including dates with the Beach Boys and Chicago. But the rest of the group were asking for more money this time. The first one had been done very much on the cheap and this, coupled with the fact that a large amount was being spent on the recordings, made them suspect that somebody was taking advantage, but the management said it was not feasible at that stage.

According to Rick, the record company had changed since The Move's American jaunt five years previously, but the company attitude had not, and they still showed a frustrating inability to promote the records. It was all rather at odds with the warm reception that the band in general and Roy in particular were getting wherever they went. They could easily have negotiated a deal, he believed, 'but tempers were frayed and it all got a bit silly.' Bob Brady said he would join the American tour, but only as long as he was paid Musicians Union rates. Rick and Keith stood by him, not out of spite against Roy, but to try and put pressure on the management. The latter told them bluntly where to go, and it was the beginning of the end.

Meanwhile, after a gap of nearly a year, in November 1975 Wizzard released *Rattlesnake Roll*, their eighth single and their first on the Jet label. Featuring Rick on pedal steel guitar, it carried on to some extent where *Ready to Rock* left off, in the pre-Phil Spector, rock'n'jive tradition of the 1950s. Its boogie-woogie piano intro even anticipated the swing revival which swept Britain by storm – well, for at least two weeks in early 1976, during a brief spell which saw articles on the subject in the tabloid press and a three-track maxi-single by the Glenn Miller Orchestra spend five weeks in the top twenty. The B-side of *Roll*, *Can't Help My Feelings*, was written by Bob Brady.

When the record was played on Radio 1's *Round Table*, an admiring John Peel commented that he would be outraged if *Rattlesnake Roll* was not a hit. But being out of the public eye for several months had not helped the band's chances, there would be no *Top Of The Pops* appearance this time, and TV and radio exposure proved minimal apart from a spot on ITV's *Supersonic*. This was destined to be Wizzard's last TV appearance, but *Supersonic* never had the hit 45-creating power of the BBC's evergreen chart show, and the single became their first total flop.

By this time, with no more hit singles or tours to keep the wages rolling in, Wizzard were effectively finished. Their third album, provisionally called 'Wizzo', was recorded mainly by Roy and those who were left, namely Rick, Mike and Charlie. In February 1976 another single, *Indiana Rainbow*, was released, credited to Roy Wood's Wizzard. As an attempt to fuse jazz with disco, it was not his best. According to the label information the instrumental B-side, *This Is the Thing (The Thing Is This)*, was from the forthcoming LP 'Wizzo'. This time radio interest was minimal, and there was no TV exposure. Jet thought the album was not commercial enough, and hot on the heels of two non-charting singles, they regarded it as a pointless exercise. A couple of tracks intended for the LP were aired on Radio 1's *Insight* in summer 1976, one programme devoted to Roy which was part of a series on different artists, but it stayed in the vaults. Mike and Charlie left what had become a much-reduced band, while Rick stayed to help Roy in the office and studio with ongoing projects, even living in a flat over the office, two hundred miles from his family. With no live work scheduled, he had no real income, and much against his inclination he felt he was turning into a secretary.

As luck would have it, the disbanding of Wizzard coincided with a decisive downturn in Roy's fortunes which resulted in his career temporarily grinding to a halt.

5. *LIFE IS WONDERFUL*

In common with other major names of the 1973 glam rock heyday, from 1976 Roy Wood found the charts increasingly hard to enter. At the end of 1974 Slade, Sweet, Gary Glitter and Suzi Quatro were still regularly reaching the Top 10 with almost every single, but during the next twelve months the law of diminishing returns set in for each of them as the peak chart positions became lower and lower. The writing was recognisably on the wall when Slade's *How Does It Feel*, in retrospect regarded as one of the best, most adventurous songs they ever recorded, broke a run of twelve consecutive top five singles, including five No. 1s, by climbing no higher than No. 15. A few weeks earlier, Sweet had seen their string of seven consecutive Top 10 hits snapped when *Turn It Down*, which had admittedly been given limited airplay by the BBC because some of its lyrical content was deemed not fit for family audiences, fizzled out at No. 41. T. Rex, whose singles had flown effortlessly into the Top 10 during the first week of release up to and including the summer of 1973, were now struggling to make the Top 30.

Times had changed, and in a changing musical climate where disco was definitely the in-flavour, and Mud seemed to be the only glam rock act who could do no wrong, Roy's next solo records likewise sold poorly. In November 1975 his second solo album 'Mustard' was released on Jet. It credited him a co-engineer as writer, producer, arranger and sleeve painter. However, it was less a solo album than 'Boulders', and included vocal contributions from Renaissance's Annie Haslam, with whom he had become romantically involved, Phil Everly, the ever-supportive Rick Price, who also took the sleeve photos, and Dick Plant. Overall 'Mustard' was less commercial than 'Boulders', and in the opinion of some it was weighed down too much by majestic ballads like *The Song* and *The Rain Came Down On Everything*. The difficult times he had been going through were evidently reflected in the music, and a sleeve note thanking the others for 'words of encouragement when they were most needed'.

The two most instant tracks, *Look Thru' The Eyes of a Fool* and *Any Old Time Will Do*, came out as singles in November 1975 and August 1976 with a spot on *Supersonic* for the former, as he mimed with saxophone in hand, but to nil effect. (*Look*, with some copies pressed as *Looking Thru' The Eyes of a Fool* on the label, had been released only five weeks after *Rattlesnake Roll*, which almost put both head-to-head and thus might have effectively scuppered the chart chances of either). Tongue-in-cheek musical parody came in *You Sure Got It Now*, which sounded like the Andrews Sisters one moment, Status Quo the next, and *Get On Down Home*, another Led Zeppelinesque piece complete with John Bonham-like drum solo.

Dick Plant was a studio engineer who worked with Roy, as well as with Jeff Lynne and ELO, over a period of many years. Both were friends and had considerable respect for each other. In the studio Roy, he said, was easy going and open to ideas from others, although nothing deterred him from his original goal.' His great strength 'was that he could, after a little practice, learn to play any instrument at all. Many times he hired things in that he would sit with for a while and then get to play quite well enough to put a part down with a few drop-ins.' When asked to compare both musicians, Dick said that Jeff was the more 'regimented' of the two; 'Roy liked to enjoy himself, probably a little too much sometimes, in the studio. Jeff was more a 'heads down and get on with it person'.

In March 1976 EMI produced a well-compiled, excellently-packaged compilation double LP on Harvest, 'The Roy Wood Story'. Sides one and two collected all The Move A-sides, the first time they had all appeared on the same record, plus *Make Them Understand* from the Mike Sheridan days, side three two of his ELO tracks plus the Wizzard A-sides, and side four his solo singles with Harvest plus two by-then unavailable B-sides. The project had Roy's blessing in the form of a handwritten message, reproduced alongside a selection of photos from all stages of his career, and a nicely objective, well-informed sleeve note from Al Clark. At the same time a three-track single containing the first three Wizzard A-sides was released, though perhaps more in hope than in expectation of chart success.

Numerous managerial issues and contractual problems grounded Roy to the extent where he was unable to work at all for a time. The few certain facts about the dark stage of his career emerged from a very guarded interview in *Melody Maker*, published in September 1977.

At one time, Roy said, he was signed to three entirely different companies (EMI, Warner Brothers, and Jet, a new label which had been set up by Don Arden in 1974), and had no idea which of these was legally entitled to issue what. Arden, who managed Roy and ELO with help from his son David and daughter Sharon, who as Sharon Osbourne would years later become equally well-known as the wife of former Black Sabbath vocalist Ozzy Osbourne and as *X Factor* panellist alongside Simon Cowell and Louis Walsh, had wanted Roy to continue producing more chart-orientated, commercial records. Roy's yearnings to get away from the pure pop side and more into jazz found no managerial approval, and professional problems spilled over into personal disagreement.

It was ironic that ELO started to duplicate their US success with lasting British chart acceptance at the end of 1975 just as Roy's records were making that unheralded trip from new release racks to bargain bins. ELO had been Roy's brainchild in the first place, and it was he who had originally invited Jeff Lynne to be a part of it. That it was Jeff's leadership which had taken them to worldwide megastardom despite their inauspicious early days was undeniable, but it pained Roy that he was not getting any credit for launching it all. To rub salt into the wound, both Jeff and Bev had made less than charitable observations on their former musical partner in a recent interview. In another Jeff, who was giving less interviews to the media by now and allowing Bev to be the main spokesman, stated firmly that Don Arden had asked him not to say anything about Roy. Compounding that, ELO had made it largely as a result of Jeff's delegating the strings on records to an orchestra, and getting Louis Clark to do the string arrangements. It was a negation of Roy's original plan that the strings should be played by the band.

Even some critics who liked ELO's work at this stage were tempted to suggest that the group would have probably been more innovative if only Roy had stayed at the helm. As ever, it is a sad fact of life that creativity and a good business brain do not always go together. Carl Wayne later remarked perceptively that Roy was always immensely gifted, but not particularly well motivated with regard to a business head. 'It's sad because a man with his talent should have been an enormously successful chap.'

For a while Roy and his closest associates felt too demoralised to form another band. Even so, there was plenty to occupy his time. Around this period he played saxophone on *Heavyhead*, an instrumental by Bev Bevan which appeared on the B-side of *Let There Be Drums*, a solo single issued by the drummer on Jet in the summer of 1976. When a soundtrack to the movie *All This And World War II* was created, using songs by John Lennon and Paul McCartney backed by the London Symphony Orchestra with vocals on specific tracks by acts including the Four Seasons, the Bee Gees, David Essex, Status Quo (or more accurately Francis Rossi on his own), Leo Sayer, Rod Stewart, Bryan Ferry, Frankie Laine, Keith Moon, Henry Gross and inevitably Jeff Lynne among others, Roy laid down vocals to very short versions of *Lovely Rita* and *Polythene Pam*.

He also did some work with Birmingham punk band the Suburban Studs. Although a number of punk performers and music journalists were going through a phase of tempting to disown almost every musical form that had existed up until then, Roy was still much admired and respected by, and a considerable influence on, many of the new wave. Some of them, it must be admitted, had a similar attitude to that of The Move in their early hell-raising days. However he did not put himself out as a producer as such, 'because I was a bit confused as to just what my role was supposed to be.' Was he supposed to lock himself away in the studio and wait for contracts to run out, or get out and play? Not surprisingly, he preferred to do the latter.

At length the contractual situation was eased. By this time he had a new group, the Wizzo Band, and signed a new deal with Warner Brothers. Wizzo was clearly what Roy had been aiming for in the final months with Wizzard, an unequivocal step into jazz which owed something to rock but distanced itself from the pop market. It had been mainly the influence of Mike Burney, Nick Pentelow and Bob Brady, who had got everyone from the old band into regular jazz blows at soundchecks during the last band's final months. Wizzo Band was something of a risk in the same way as ELO Mk I had been, but it was one that Roy wanted to take, on the grounds that it was 'the sort of music that I can be playing when I'm 50, I can't be a pop singer all my life.'

After all, as he said, jazz-rock was nothing new. Musicians like Stanley Clarke and Chick Corea had been experimenting with rock, but what was rare was to find it the other way around, with rock bands getting into jazz. While he was unable to work during the previous months, he had frequented jazz clubs in Birmingham learning jazz guitar. It did him good as a writer, he felt, as it taught him more about different chord progressions. In his words, Wizzo Band had a very heavy, 'almost Zeppelinish' rhythm section, 'and the songs are very commercial, so it makes for quite an interesting combination'.

The Wizzo Band made their debut on BBC TV/Radio 1's *Sight And Sound In Concert* on 2 April 1977. They comprised a hefty brass section, plus newcomers Graham Gallery on bass and Dave Donovan on drums. Rick Price proved his versatility by playing the steel guitar which he had unveiled on *Rattlesnake Roll*. As for appearances, Roy had discarded his warpaint and taken to donning boldly-striped legwarmers instead.

From the opening bars of the first number, *Life Is Wonderful*, it was clear that here was a very different Roy Wood from the one most people had seen or heard, with the repertoire consisted of lengthy jazz-funk pieces which must have surprised fans who had followed him since the early days. Likewise the band, sitting in front of their music stands, all gave the impression of a far more disciplined ensemble than the splendidly chaotic, pantomime-like Wizzard. Nonetheless the programme should have been the perfect launch pad to put him back in the public eye after having been largely absent from TV and radio with new releases for a while. Some of the pieces would appear on the forthcoming album, while another song, *French Perfume*, was introduced as from the unreleased Wizzard LP sessions. The only familiar numbers were the Wizzard rearrangement of *California Man* interpolating the riff from *Brontosaurus*, and as a finale *Are You Ready to Rock*.

Sadly for Roy's enthusiasm, their first gig was their only one. While ELO were taking up what appeared to be permanent residence in the LP chart and had one Top 10 single after another (although a solo disco single by Jeff Lynne, *Doin' That Crazy Thing,* received very little airplay and sank without trace), and while an over-excitable media preened itself during the long hot summer of punk/new wave for the increasingly outrageous antics of punk rock bands in general and the Sex Pistols in particular, Wizzo were completely ignored.

Two singles, *The Stroll*, released in the summer and *Dancin' At The Rainbow's End*, which appeared early the following year, met with largely indifferent, rather bemused reviews and no airplay, as did the LP 'Super Active Wizzo', released in the autumn. The latter consisted of three lengthy tracks per side, only two clocking in at less than six minutes each, and two breaking the eleven-minute barrier. Four were written by Roy on his own, another a collaboration with Annie Haslam, and Dave Donovan, and another featured lyrics co-written by Roy with Dick Plant.

But it all failed to resonate with the public, let alone the media. 'In no way is it super active, more bleach boring,' ran a review in *Record Mirror*, which went on to comment on its 'six tortuously unoriginal 'jazzy' tracks with the odd strained vocal tossed on to a heap of clumsy brass and guitar concoctions'. Many fans would later agree with the verdict of the All Music Guide website that 'Super Active Wizzo' was 'perhaps the weakest single LP ever to bear Roy Wood's name'.

Early in 1978 a British tour was scheduled, but the odds against taking such a large and expensive, and as yet zero-charting, outfit on the road were overwhelming, and it was cancelled before a single date was played. Warner Bros were not impressed with the Band or concept, but the band carried on rehearsing until Rick could no longer afford to keep going. When he left, 'it went down the drain.' 'You know the saying, "Play jazz and starve," Roy commented in retrospect. 'I think that sums it up. But I would really like to have done it. ELO were a fusion of classical and pop, this would have been a fusion of jazz and pop. Mike Burney, the sax player from Wizzard, went on to join the Syd Lawrence Orchestra, so I had the musos around me to do it.'

Others did not see it from that point of view. David Arden, Don's son, at Jet Records, told him that he was going in the wrong direction with the jazz. The most sensible thing to do would be to cut everything back, and slim down the personnel to a neat three-piece combo. He later revealed that a plan was set up for Roy to form an outfit along these lines with a couple of name rock musicians, whose names however could not be divulged as the groups they were with at the time had no idea of the impending scheme, and they were still with the same bands ten years later.

Roy found his record and management company's outlook and lack of interest in his new plans very shortsighted. To him it was an attitude that smacked of 'Come back when you've got another *See My Baby Jive*'. How, he asked, could anybody be expected to work under that kind of pressure? The media, he reckoned, never took the concept of the Wizzo Band that seriously, and dismissed it out of hand as another wild idea which was never going to work, largely because it was totally at odds with the public's perception of him as a pop star and what everybody expected from his name on the record label. He might however have recalled the experience of Manfred Mann, who had disbanded what Manfred himself regarded contemptuously as his pop hit single factory in 1969 to form the experimental, more worthy jazz-rock combo Manfred Mann Chapter Three. This only lasted for two poorly-selling albums and less than two years, before bowing to the inevitable and reverting to more mainstream, more successful pop/rock under the name of Manfred Mann's Earthband. Coincidentally, like ELO they had on occasion looked to the classics for a little inspiration. Only a few months after Jeff and group had gone Top 10 by creating a fusion of Chuck Berry and Beethoven's Fifth Symphony, Manfred Mann's Earthband enjoyed the first of their only three Top 10 hits with *Joybringer*, which leant heavily on a movement from Holst's *The Planets*.

Around this time a chance meeting led to a meeting between Roy and Annie Haslam, vocalist with Renaissance, who coincidentally were also signed to Warner Bros. They had just been recording their new album at De Lane Lea Studios, Wembley. On one of their days off Dick Plant, who was engineering the record, invited her to come over and meet him. This in turn resulted in her recording a solo LP 'Annie in Wonderland', which featured Roy throughout as producer and arranger. Jon Camp, who played bass with Renaissance and wrote two of the tracks, Dave Donovan and Louis Clark, likewise contributed to and played on much of it. But as was perhaps only to be expected, Roy played most of the instruments as well as arranging, producing and designing the sleeve, as befitting the title, a painting featuring the Mad Hatter and other characters from the stories of Lewis Carroll. He wrote three of the tracks specially for the project. One, *I Never Believed In Love*, was recorded as a duet between them, and released as a single. It was perhaps the most instant track on a very eclectic album which also included such varied fare as Rodgers & Hammerstein's *If I Loved You* and the old jazz standard *Nature Boy*.

If I Loved You featured Roy coming up with yet another unusual sound. At the time he had found a shop in London which was having a sale of instruments at reduced prices, and he thus acquired two balalaikas, one with eight strings and another with three. On their own, he said, they sounded odd, but together the result was 'fantastic', and they provided the basis for a one-man, multi-tracked balalaika orchestra. On an instrumental section which he wrote for the middle of the song, he lifted the lid of the grand piano and played the strings with large Allen keys. As if such inventiveness was not enough, he then enhanced the effect by putting a fire extinguisher on the loud pedal of the grand piano, 'so the strings were loud all the time - and it worked really really well'.

While they were recording the album, they met Paul and Linda McCartney and Denny Laine, who were in a neighbouring studio working on 'Wings At The Speed Of Sound'. Paul immediately wanted to know whose voice he had been hearing, 'as it was sending shivers down my spine'. They visited Roy and Annie in their studio and chatted about music for a couple of hours, although no musical collaborations between Roy and the former Beatle and his group were forthcoming.

For Annie, the album was a tremendous experience, on which they tried out jazz, pop, rock, 'and a lot of fun things, like African drums'. She said afterwards that she learned a great deal from Roy when it came to working in the studio, particularly when treble-tracking her voice on lead lines and not just choruses. Sometimes they would be laughing so much in the studio that they would be on their hands and knees on the floor, crying helplessly. On other occasions she would be doing her vocal behind a screen, totally oblivious to the fooling around by Roy and the engineers. She would come out to find them sitting there with paper plates on their heads, holding numbers up to say what her points were. One track, *Going Home*, included a Welsh male voice choir, whom they did not have to pay for their work, but only needed to supply with beer afterwards.

Two of the songs which would later be recorded by Renaissance were indirectly inspired by Roy. *Trip To The Fair*, written by John Tout and Michael Dunford from the band and lyricist Betty Thatcher, was about a visit Annie, Roy, Dick and his wife made to a fair at Hampstead one bank holiday while they were taking a break from recording, after they had had lunch together and ended up eating the gardenias in the drinks, as 'you do that when you're with Roy'. Sadly the fair was closed by the time they arrived. The other, *Northern Lights*, written by Dunford and Thatcher, was partly about Annie's feelings after spending time with Roy and missing him while they were apart. She suggested treble-tracking the main melody line, 'which completely changed the whole feel of the song'. The hard work paid off, for in the summer of 1978 it would become Renaissance's only hit single, reaching No. 10.

6. ROCK CITY

After the demise of the Wizzo Band, Roy switched to Automatic Records. A small shortlived label within Warner Bros, it had been set up by Nick Mobbs, whom Roy had known since he was head of Harvest Records and then an A&R man with EMI, largely responsible for the Sex Pistols' signing briefly with the latter company until the controversies made them too hot to handle. Staying with Warners and being on Nick's label, he said, would ease a lot of problems. The only musician left from the Wizzo line-up was keyboard player and guitarist Paul Robbins, who brought his old friend, bassist Pete Mackie. Joined by saxophonist Billy Paul from Wizzo, they went to make a new album at Rockfield Studios, Monmouth.

The tracks they recorded included a guest appearance from the man whom Roy rated as his favourite musician of all time, the one who might have filled the drum stool when The Move were originally formed. Led Zeppelin were rehearsing at Clearwell Castle nearby, and looking for somewhere to record their next and what would be their final album, 'In Through The Out Door'. They came to look at Rockfield, found Roy there, 'and we all had a bit of a laugh'. Roy was playing drums, and he mentioned that they did not have a drummer. John Bonham said he was bored with rehearsals, and Roy invited him to play on one of the tracks. He promised he would be back next day, and kept his word, returning with Robert Plant to add his contribution to *Keep Your Hands On The Wheel*. The same song, boasting backing vocals from Carl Wayne, the first appearance he had made on one of Roy's records since leaving The Move, was released as a single on Warner Bros in November 1978.

Sadly, by then the days of the hard-drinking Bonham were numbered. He died in September 1980, and Roy, Jeff and Bev were once again united, being among those who attended his funeral at St Michael's Church, Rushock, Worcestershire, on 10 October. They were squeezed in at the back of the small church, a miserable occasion which Bev later described as perhaps the saddest, most horrible funeral he had ever attended.

(We're) On The Road Again, one of the first on WEA's new Automatic label and also a limited edition picture disc in the summer of 1979, included Andy Fairweather-Low on backing vocals, and Paul Robbins on Roland JP4 synthesiser and clavinet. The song's arrangement included not just Roy's beloved celli and tenor, alto and baritone saxes, but also a rhythm track which would not have made it out of place in a chart which included disco-orientated fare from the likes of Gloria Gaynor, Amii Stewart and Dan Hartman. Even acts such as Rod Stewart, Paul McCartney and the Beach Boys had recently scored heavily, or as some might have it revived what could have otherwise threatened to become flagging careers, with singles that had followed in the footsteps of the Bee Gees, *Jive Talkin'* onwards, and tipped their hats to the disco phenomenon. The B-side of the single, *Saxmaniacs*, an instrumental, was credited to 'The Midlands Horns' – Roy, Nick Pentelow and Mike Burney, another unreleased track from Wizzard's latter days. The snappy title had originally been a little longer than one word – *Don't Nick My Pentelow Or You Mike Get Burneyed*.

Ironically, 1979 heralded a sharp rise in the price of oil and related products, and with it a threat of vinyl shortages, although the craze for coloured vinyl, picture discs and 12" singles went on unabated. Roy's third solo LP, 'On The Road Again', was only released in the US and Europe, and therefore only obtainable briefly in Britain as an import. It had a troubled history at home, for the finished tapes were taken to Nick Mobbs, but as the contract was with Warners, he had a limited say as to its release. Becoming ultra-critical, he played the album to himself every day in his office and to his friends, getting to the point where he thought it was somehow wrong, and in the process Roy began to question himself about it. Eventually Nick asked Roy to change three of the tracks which he did not like. Roy did change the tracks – but still the album was never released in Britain. The US arm of Warner Bros only put it out after Roy and his personal assistant Richard Battle went there for a short holiday and paid a personal visit to the label's headquarters.

A much more upbeat, lively set than 'Mustard', it featured extended versions of the last two singles, plus *Dancin' At The Rainbow's End*, which had been the second Wizzo Band 45. It was less of a solo LP than its predecessors, as all ten tracks included other musicians, among them three members of the Wizzo Band, namely Dave Donovan, Paul Robbins, and Billy Paul, plus Charlie Grima from Wizzard, and not surprisingly Annie Haslam. In mood the songs embraced jazz-rock (*Another Night, Colourful Lady*), straightforward rock'n'roll (*Road Rocket*), rock *(Backtown Sinner),* and folk (*Wings Over the Sea, Jimmy Lad*). *Wings Over the Sea* might have been intended as an affectionate pun. Roy hosted an edition of Radio 1's *Star Special* early in 1980, in which he DJ'ed his way through two hours of his favourite records. Among them was Wings' *Mull of Kintyre*, which gave him a chance to say how much he loved the song.

The Move were still fondly remembered in some quarters, not least by a new generation of bands. In Britain, Paul Weller of the Jam and later the Style Council was an ardent admirer of their back catalogue, especially of songs like *Blackberry Way* and *Beautiful Daughter*. Other names such as Adam Ant and Aztec Camera's Roddy Frame also paid tribute to his influence. On the other side of the Atlantic, Cheap Trick were devoted fans. In 1978 they covered *California Man*, with a few seconds of the *Brontosaurus* riff as a single, and in 1990 a subsequent album 'Busted' included their version of *We're Gonna Rock'n'Roll Tonight*. Roy cheerfully repaid the admiration by making occasional surprise appearances onstage and in the studio with the band. The first was at Barbarella's, Birmingham and the second at Hammersmith Odeon, both in February 1979, the latter also featuring Dave Edmunds who found himself sharing a mic with Roy. Seven years later Roy contributed backing vocals to a Cheap Trick song *Money Is The Route Of All Fun*. In 1993 he co-wrote a couple of songs with their vocalist Robin Zander, for the latter's planned solo album, a project which would remain unreleased.

As with constant speculation throughout the 1970s of a possible reunion by the Beatles, there was talk from time to time of The Move getting together again – even if only in the wildest speculation by fans and music journalists. Nevertheless there was a one-off charity gig at the Birmingham Locarno around 1979 when Roy, Bev, Mike Hopkins and Ace Kefford on a borrowed bass got together for a short set including *I Can Hear The Grass Grow, California Man* and *Watch Your Step*. Ace, who sang on the latter, admitted that it 'sounded terrible, but it was a lot of fun'. It was the first time he had seen Roy and Bev for several years, and the latter told him that in his opinion, after Ace left, 'The Move had gone down the tubes'.

Though his own records were barely selling any more by the end of the decade, Roy was still in demand as a producer for others. His name appeared in this capacity on singles by the Paranoids, *Love Job*, and P45, *Right Direction*. Due to lack of time, a request by Def Leppard to produce their first album had to be turned down. His most successful work as a producer was for Darts, who established themselves as Britain's most consistent doo-wop rock'n'roll revivalists towards the end of the decade. The resulting LP 'Dart Attack', which he also co-arranged with the group as well as contributing guitar, cello, sax and banjo, spawned three hit singles, the summer 1979 top tenner *Duke of Earl*, and its much less successful follow-ups later that year *Can't Get Enough Of Your Love*, and *Reet Petite*.

Darts sax player Nigel Trubridge found Roy 'light years ahead of anybody else I had ever worked with' in terms of production, as well as great fun to work with. He was particularly impressed with Roy's recreation of the Spector wall of sound, as well as his ability to get a Clarence Clemons-like rasp from the tenor sax. However, the venture was not without a few problems between band and producer.

As it was not his own band and he was the hired hand, they had different ways of working which were not always compatible. The members of Darts would arrive at the studio about midday and work on things before Roy arrived at around five o'clock in the afternoon, 'would mope around' and listen to what they had been working on last, then suggested they all went out to eat. Returning to the studio at ten o'clock, he would mix himself an enormous Scotch and coke and say, 'right let's go'. By two o'clock next morning they were ready to add the vocals, but Darts did not really feel up to doing close vocal harmonies at that time in the morning, so compromises were called for.

Roy also had difficulties with the fact that everyone in the band wanted a say, as did the manager, and the guy from the record company. 'All of a sudden you've got a room full of people, and you can't concentrate any more and you can't produce like you were hired to do'. Sometimes, he felt, there was no alternative to saying, 'Just clear off for a bit, so I can do it, *then* you can hear it!' Some members of the band felt rather sidelined during the sessions, compromised by his enthusiasm and insistence on doing things his own way, while the others were happy to let him have free rein. Moreover, the album marked a decline in Darts' selling power. Their first three albums, one a somewhat premature greatest hits compilation, had all sold enough to reach the Top 20 (two making the Top 10) and staying in the charts for several months, but *Dart Attack* rose no higher than No. 38 during a four-week run.

As a musician, at this time Roy also guested on sitar on an instrumental album written, arranged and conducted by Louis Clark, '(per-spek-tiv)n'. Released in March 1979, it was a project which reunited him briefly with Nick Pentelow from Wizzard, while John Tout from Renaissance, and several members of Sky, including Francis Monkman and Kevin Peek, also played on the sessions.

This coincided with stories in the music press of Roy forming a new band for live gigs, tentatively called Rock Brigade. In the event, this remained no more than a moniker for the assortment of friends who had accompanied him on the solo LP. It was a difficult time for Roy, who did not have a manager, only an accountant. By the early 1980s recording deals were increasingly hard to come by, even for established names whose records had been flying out of the shops on release three or four years previously. The combined effects of major record companies having spent (if not overspent) massively on punk bands who were the darlings of the trendy music weeklies but came nowhere near recouping their advances as their records simply did not sell enough, plus a new recession, a near doubling in the rate of VAT from 8% to 15% in the incoming Conservative government's budget of June 1979, and a downturn in record sales, all combined to send a chill through an industry which had seen a golden era and was about to experience a cold new morning.

Sitting on the other side of the control desk, Roy did some work at the Old Smithy Studios, near his home patch in Worcestershire, and talking to the owner about recording some of his own material there without being sure of what was going to happen to it. The last thing he wanted was to be in a position where he was hawking new product around to every major label, as it would look unprofessional. His accountant advised him to do a one-off so that people could see that he had a record out and was still doing something.

The result was *Rock City*, credited on the sleeve and label to Helicopters (Roy Wood), which appeared in November 1980 via Cheapskate Records, an independent label run by Chas Chandler, Slade manager, and Frank Lea, brother of Slade's bass guitarist and violinist Jim Lea. The timing was perfect, as a club called Rock City had just opened in Nottingham, and the management adopted it as their theme music. While Roy was promoting the single, Radio 1 was doing a week in Birmingham, something with which he was obviously glad to be involved. 'It was through sheer exasperation that *Rock City* got played on Radio 1,' he said. Cheapskate had just released it but, perhaps in keeping with their name, were not promoting it at all. Roy and Richard Battle were on their way to Edinburgh when the car broke down and they returned to Birmingham, where the Radio 1 presenters had teamed up with the local Top Rank Club DJs. Despite misgivings that it might seem a little pushy of him, Roy went in, determined to promote the record himself, and they all welcomed him with open arms. He went backstage, was invited to a party afterwards, got chatting, and the record was duly played on air. Simon Bates invited Roy on to his mid-morning show next day on which he played a bit of classical guitar and bagpipes live.

'Things seemed to be going my way after three years of feeling I'd been knocking my head against a brick wall,' he remarked. 'I've always known what direction I wanted to go in and aimed for it, but I got involved with so many people who confused me that I ended up not knowing what to write or what sort of band to form. That's why I went into production – to cool off.'

Cheapskate also released a seasonal solo single, *Sing Out The Old, Bring In The New*, a song which had originally written for and recorded by Darts during the 'Dart Attack' sessions but not issued at the time (and in fact, not till the remastered CD appeared in 2011 when it surfaced as a bonus track), a month later. Neither this nor *Rock City* ever breached the charts, but the name Helicopters would live on for a while. After Roy had recorded with Annie Haslam and produced her solo album, he was talking to Jon Camp of Renaissance, who suggested they form a part-time band together for occasional college gigs. The initial line-up included Roy on lead vocals, guitar, saxes and bagpipes, Jon on bass, Paul Robbins on guitar and keyboards or Mike Deacon from Darts on keyboards, and Kex Gorin from Magnum on drums.

As all the latter were playing in other bands at the same time, it was difficult to gather everyone for rehearsals, and Roy made up cassettes of the stuff in their repertoire so that each member could learn at home, then get together for a couple of days, while gigs had to be fitted around whenever they were free; 'it was just a way of getting on stage and doing something.' They made their London debut with two consecutive nights at the Marquee on 14 and 15 December, and played the Venue two months later. Their repertoire generally included the new singles which Roy was recording at around this time, a medley of Move hits, plus *10538 Overture* and some of the Wizzard singles, including invariably *I Wish it Could Be Christmas Everyday*, regardless of what time of year it might be, the old Little Richard standard *Keep A'Knockin'*. A newer song which featured in the set was *Backtown Sinner*, from what Roy referred to as 'the American album' when introducing it on stage, with Paul Robbins handling lead vocals.

One fan who saw the band at both gigs was author Miles Tredinnick, who under the showbiz alias of Riff Regan had been vocalist with London, a new wave band which had split in 1978 (only to reform thirty years later), and had recently embarked on a solo career. On the second occasion he went with his friend Alan Heywood, who was Roy's accountant at the time. After the show, Alan took him to the dressing room under the stage and introduced them both. Miles told him what a great gig it had been. 'You liked it, then?' Roy replied, as if relieved to be reassured that it had gone well. It amazed Miles, who had met several other equally famous names in the business, that somebody of Roy's standing was so genuinely modest and self-effacing.

Early in 1981 Roy returned to EMI Records for the first time in seven years, with a two-single deal. In April he released a 45 credited to Roy Wood's Helicopters, *Green Glass Windows*, featuring the Kempsey School Choir, who had also sung on *Sing Out The Old*. The B-side, *The Driving Song*, featured Noddy Holder on backing vocals, albeit well down in the mix. It was followed at the end of the month by another solo outing *Down to Zero*, backed with the instrumental *Olympic Flyer*.

Yet it was not to be either of these singles that put Roy back in the charts for the first time in six years. In December a reissue of *I Wish it Could be Christmas Everyday*, backed with *See My Baby Jive*, saw Wizzard return to *Top Of The Pops* and the Top 50, peaking at No. 41. It was fitting that one of the best-ever seasonal singles should have become as much a Yuletide classic as Slade's 1973 evergreen *Merry Xmas Everybody*.

In February 1982 another solo single, *It's Not Easy,* backed with *Moonriser,* hit the shops, but the title must have seemed appropriate. Mike Read, who was presenting the Radio 1 breakfast show at the time, had always been a fervent supporter of Roy and his music, and played the record several times, but not even this could push it into the Top 75. Around the same time Helicopters, with Roy and Jon now joined by Robin George on guitar, Tom Farnell from Fairport Convention on drums, and Terry Rowley on keyboards, recorded a live album at the Marquee provisionally for release through Cheapskate, but Roy decided he would shelve it until they had had some success with a view to putting it out on EMI. Sadly, the shelf was where it remained.

A third single for EMI, *Aerial Pictures*, backed with *Airborne*, was recorded for subsequent single release in summer 1982. Roy had wanted it to be his first single on EMI and also thought it might be a good title track for a Helicopters album, but owing to the lack of success with its predecessors it was cancelled. Convinced that it was too good to tuck away, Roy took the backing track to Carl Wayne, who added his vocals. The result, backed with a new version of Roy's *Colourful Lady* from the 1979 LP, was released as a single on the Jet label, credited to Charlie Wayne. The writer's own recordings of both songs eventually appeared in 2006 on an EMI compilation 'Roy Wood the Wizzard!'

Although he had left The Move under less than amicable circumstances, Carl had always remained the best of friends with Roy over the years. In an interview some years later with Martin Kinch on Stoke Mandeville Hospital Radio, he said he had always been Roy's greatest fan, and when asked to choose his favourite Move single, he named *Chinatown*, even though it was one of those recorded after his departure. He was generous with his praise for the 'new Move' from 1970 to 1972 which had been the result of his leaving, and had nothing but admiration for Jeff Lynne, whom he regarded as 'a brilliant producer'. When Roy and Jeff got together in the band, 'it was the best Move of all and they had the ability to go alongside Lennon and McCartney.' ELO, with whom Carl had recorded three tracks in 1973 (which were finally released in 2003 on the thirtieth anniversary remastering and reissue of 'ELO 2', a limited edition double CD), were likewise brilliant. He was however less impressed by Wizzard, while acknowledging they were 'a great commercial band', in similar vein to their contemporaries Mud and Gary Glitter.

By the following year, Roy was in the same position as several other once-successful rock names without a recording contract in a leaner, recession-conscious UK entertainment industry. The previous year, EMI had slimmed its artist roster down almost overnight to a fraction of its former self – according to one estimate, all but 40 of its 180 names were politely shown the proverbial door. So it was back to the indie labels, and a couple of releases on the short-lived Speed outlet. In March he appeared on the alternative late-night comedy show *O.T.T.* alongside Chris Tarrant, Lenny Henry and others with a specially-written number for the programme, issued as a single. The B-side, *Mystery Song*, or so the label called it, was the Wizzo Band's *Sight and Sound In Concert* performance of *California Man/Brontosaurus*.

Woody/Speed also issued a compilation LP, 'The Singles' later that summer. Containing Move, Wizzard, Helicopters and solo work, the packaging was far inferior to that of Harvest's 'The Roy Wood Story'. There was no indication on label or sleeve as to which name the tracks had first appeared, which must have been confusing to anyone who had not followed Roy since his chart days. But it was refreshing to see a set which included some of the recent ignored cuts, and despite little publicity it sold surprisingly well, reaching No. 37 in the LP chart. It proved beyond doubt that Roy still had a strong fan base.

Further surprise guest appearances on record and stage came about when Roy took part in a Beatles concert at the Royal Albert Hall on 13 December 1982, attended by Queen Elizabeth II, the Duke of Edinburgh, and Paul and Linda McCartney. With the Royal Philharmonic Orchestra conducted by Louis Clark, he played bagpipes on *Mull of Kintyre* and *Happy Christmas (War Is Over)*. Early the following year 'Arrested', a tribute to the music of the Police, was released, again with the Royal Philharmonic, this time conducted by Don Airey. Roy's contribution was as vocalist on *Message In A Bottle*, alongside Ian Paice on drums, Neil Murray on bass and Gary Moore on guitars.

At Christmas 1983 Roy unleashed a one-off project by the Rockers, a group featuring himself with the recently disbanded Thin Lizzy's Phil Lynott, Chas Hodges of Chas and Dave, and drummer John Coghlan, who had recently left Status Quo. *We Are The Boys (Who Make All The Noise)* was a rock'n'roll medley single on CBS with Roy, Phil and Chas sharing lead vocals on songs like *Johnny B. Goode, It'll Be Me, Way Down Yonder in New Orleans*, and *Something Else*. Despite hostile reviews it got more airplay than Roy's last few singles, again largely thanks to the support of Mike Read on Radio 1, and charted modestly at No. 79.

This paled into insignificance beside the reissue in November 1984 of *I Wish It Could Be Christmas Everyday*, with a new Dennis the Menace-style cartoon sleeve of Roy's design and a 12" extended party mix. It gave him his first Top 30 showing for nearly a decade, peaking at No. 23. On the week it moved up the charts from a new entry position of No. 50 to No. 36, Roy was the first act on *Top Of The Pops*, albeit appearing as a soloist rather than with the group.

This long-overdue reappearance in the charts should have been a good springboard for his return to the recording scene on the new Legacy label. In summer 1985 the first fruits of this, *Under Fire*, with its electronic drums an intriguingly contemporary sound, made its appearance. A video was shot at Bridgnorth, Shropshire, with supporting cast in military uniform including Bev Bevan, Jim Davidson, and UB40's Norman Hassan. The B-side, *On Top Of the World*, featured a stirring string arrangement by Louis Clark, whose work in a similar guise had made him as good as a full member of ELO. Legacy did the full honours with an extended version of the A-side on a 12" single, and giving away water pistols with initial copies of the 7". In November came a remake of *Sing Out The Old...Bring In The New*, featuring the Kempsey School Choir, again on 7" and 12", the latter featuring three different mixes. A few promo copies of the 7" single with pop-up Christmas card, signed by Roy, were distributed to the media, although plans to make this format widely available to the general release were abandoned because of cost. Nevertheless, for all Legacy's promotional activities, Radio 1 proved unresponsive, and without airplay there was no way they could bring about a full-scale revival of Roy's chart career.

Ironically it coincided with what had probably been Roy's best media exposure for the last ten years. On 15 March 1986 Heartbeat'86, a children's hospital charity fund-raising venture, staged an all-star gig at Birmingham National Exhibition Centre, a line-up including ELO, the Moody Blues, the Rockin' Berries, UB40, the Fortunes, the Applejacks, the Steve Gibbons Band, Robert Plant – and, according to advance publicity, The Move. It had been rumoured that the occasion would see a partial reformation of the group, and the media eagerly announced this as if it was a fait accompli. According to Ace, the stumbling block was Roy, who had wanted Rick Price to join them again on bass for the occasion.

Roy's recollection of events was a little different. After years of 'being stuck in the studio, beginning to feel a bit claustrophobic', he jumped at the chance to return to live performances. When he received a phone call asking him to join the bill, he said yes and put the phone down, having forgotten that he was without a band at the time. A few further calls to friends and musicians, and a suggestion from one that they get together an all-girl brass section, resulted in a rehearsal where they blew him away; 'it was unbelievable'. No more was heard of a reconstituted Move.

Roy and his new band played an hour-long set, including an appearance by the Kempsey School Choir on *Green Glass Windows*. The capacity crowd of 11,500 gave them a five-minute standing ovation, and he told the local press that after he came offstage he nearly broke down and cried, as it had been a long time since he had played for such a marvellous crowd. Several people in the audience maintained that he had stolen the show, which raised £200,000. It was followed by a compilation of tracks from various associated artists, 'Action!', on the Midlands-based FM label, with proceeds going to the same hospital charity. Among the songs included on it was *Green Glass Windows*.

A two-hour selection of highlights was shown on BBC TV in August, featuring three numbers from Roy's set, in addition to the finale in which he joined most of the other acts onstage plus George

Harrison, Dave Edmunds, Noddy Holder and Denny Laine on guitars and shared vocals, plus a host of others, Ace Kefford on tambourine among them, for *Johnny B. Goode*. Though it was not the beginning of an upturn in his career that it might have been, at least it marked the start of The Roy Wood Big Band.

The Heartbeat 86 fund-raising activities were wound up in September 1987, by which time over £700,000 had been raised for the hospital. To mark the occasion, Roy and Bev were among those present at the opening of a covered walkway at the hospital.

His fourth solo album was initially to be called 'Imminent Attack' before being changed to 'Starting Up'. Recorded at UB40's Birmingham studio, it hit the record shops at the end of the year. At first glance, with titles like *Red Cars Are After Me*, and the more jazz-funk *Hot Cars* it seemed in part like a concept album on motors; 'I had a few songs on the shelf that were all sort of connected to cars and I put them all together.' The title track opened with the sound of a key being turned in the ignition, and was given added colour part of the way through by a sitar break. A single, the melancholy, reflective *Raining In The City*, was released at the same time.

Yet a lack of promotion and zero media interest doomed single and album, and those who eagerly scanned the charts week after week in the hope that their hero might be back in business would be disappointed. Roy said he had the feeling that Legacy were using the album as a tax loss; 'they paid for the recording costs but very little else.' The finished product did not come up to his expectations. He recorded it without Dolby noise reduction as he felt it sounded warmer with a bit of analog tape hiss, but when the album was mastered they added it, 'and to me it made it sound all digitised and electronic and horrible. It took the warmth out of it and I can't actually listen to it any more.' With hindsight, though, the consensus of critical opinion suggests that on the whole the material on 'Starting Up' did not measure up to the standards of the material on the first two, even three solo albums.

Nevertheless it was all the more disappointing as he had been given some exposure thanks to another young and briefly successful group who had long been admirers. In the summer of 1986 Doctor and the Medics had begun their chart career with a chart-topping cover of Norman Greenbaum's *Spirit In The Sky* and followed it up with a less successful, but still Top 30, hit from their own stable. In the autumn they recorded a new version of ABBA's 1974 Eurovision winner *Waterloo*. The song's composers, Benny Andersson, Bjorn Ulvaeus and Stig Anderson, admitted that one of their major inspirations at the time had been *See My Baby Jive*, and now Doctor and the Medics repaid the compliment by issuing a cover version with Roy Wood on backing vocals and saxophone. Several TV appearances, including *Cheggers Plays Pop* and *Saturday Superstore* followed, to say nothing of a hilarious Eurovision spoof video in which the group and Roy appeared miming the song, interspersed with Katie Boyle reprising her role as Eurovision song contest compere while choking on clouds of dry ice, and various guests including Lemmy of Motorhead and Captain Sensible of the Damned, holding up score cards as part of the voting panel. Yet the record received a bad press from reviewers and radio presenters, who failed to see the funny side of what was surely one of the best-executed musical jokes of its time, and a four-week stint in the Top 75 saw it go no higher than No. 45.

What might have been another small boost to his career came at the same time when soul band Buddy Curtess and the Grasshoppers recorded and issued their own version of *Hello Susie* on a single at around the same time. Once again there was some TV exposure, but very little airplay and once again no chart action.

'Starting Up' marked the end of Roy's brief stint with Legacy. Meanwhile the Ardens at Jet Records had always kept in touch with him, and in 1987 he went to them with a new recording. Uncharacteristically it was a cover version, a rough take of Len Barry's 1965 bubblegum No. 2 hit, *1-2-3*. This, they thought, could be the record to get him back into the public eye. (The Communards, Kim Wilde and George Harrison were all enjoying their greatest successes around this time with revamped oldies, both of the latter peaking at No. 2 in Britain and No. 1 the other side of the Atlantic). With Nick Pentelow on sax, the finished recording was released in the summer, available in 7" and extended 12" formats. Yet once again, lack of exposure zeroed its chances of success, and it proved to be no more than a one-off deal.

In retrospect a long-term Jet contract might have been the ideal solution. Since Wizzard disbanded, Roy's career had been very much stop-go, rarely in the public eye for long at a time. Arden recognised that he had reached the stage in his career where he had been around so long that he had become something of a celebrity, but like Cliff Richard and others, sometimes found it difficult for radio to welcome new releases with open arms, because of something of an inbuilt bias against 'heritage' acts and a keenness to promote new talent instead. In the case of Cliff Richard, whose record contract with EMI was a long-lasting affair stretching over several decades with no more than the occasional pause for renegotiation, and which ensured new singles and albums at regular intervals for the ever-faithful fan base, the problem was less acute. With Roy it was a different matter. Jet wanted and needed to develop the young talent, but in spite of that, Arden was optimistic that something would come along in the not too distant future involving Roy, and they would gladly work with him on that; 'he's a great fella, great talent, and it's only a matter of time.' In fact time was not on the side of Jet Records, which closed operations in 1991.

Roy's only subsequent new appearance on record during the last years of the 1980s was as guest vocalist on *Custer's Last Stand*, a concept album by Rick Wakeman, 'Time Machine', in 1988. Lifted as a single, it went the same way as the others. However he did appear briefly on a No. 1 single in December 1989 when Jive Bunny & The Master Mixers, a studio project which briefly dominated the charts with singles which were basically compilations assembled from brief excerpts of other artists' hits set to a common percussion track, topped the charts for one week with *Let's Party*, featuring verses from the Christmas hits by Wizzard, Slade and Gary Glitter's 1984 Top 10 *Another Rock'n'Roll Christmas*.

7. LION'S HEART

Though the charts proved a mainly barren period for him from 1985 to 1995, Roy was by this time being introduced to a new audience who were barely old enough to remember Wizzard, let alone The Move. A casual glance at the television schedules would see him making appearances from time to time on shows such as *The Tube, Little And Large*, Noel Edmonds' *The Time Of Your Life*, and Mike Read's *Pop Quiz*. In January 1987 he was a guest on Radio 1's *Round Table*, a weekly show in which guests, normally including one musician or singer and one of the station's DJs, discussed the best of the week's new releases, and he reserved his greatest praise for a new single by Lone Justice, *I Found Love*.

Embracing the multi-media world, he recorded *Off The Record*, an instruction video on the use of modern recording equipment, enlivened by his customary dry humour and an otherwise unreleased song, *If This Love Is Magic*. It was one of several numbers he had recorded during this period but at the time of writing have never been made available on vinyl or CD.

Two others were the fruits of a session in 1989 with Jeff Lynne, when he went to stay at the latter's house. *Me And You*, which he described as 'an out-and-out pop song', and *If You Can't Get What You Want, You've Gotta Want What You Get*, a skiffle number, were both numbers which developed from ideas thrown in by each of them. 'I had the skeleton for *Me And You*. I took it over to Jeff's house, and played it to him, and he added some bits of his own to it as well. We did that, and whilst I was there, we stayed up all night and played a bit of skiffle, and this is how the other one came about.' With the exception of those two short throwaway tracks at the end of the third and fourth Move albums, it was the first time that both had collaborated as songwriters. Their finished efforts were duly recorded - but frustratingly both remained in the can.

By this time Jeff had disbanded ELO, which bowed out with a final live show in 1986 a few months after the Heartbeat extravaganza and what would be their last new album 'Balance Of

Power', packaged in a lacklustre sleeve, in terms of playing time their shortest and in chart statistics their least successful (one week in the Top 10, and only one Top 30 single) since the non-charting 'Face The Music' in 1975. It had been made by the three-piece band, Jeff playing most of the instruments as well as handling all vocals, Bev on drums and Richard Tandy on keyboards, with no string players, and a session saxophonist, Christian Schneider, on one track. A little later he would embark on a new phase of his career which saw him produce a triumphant comeback album for George Harrison in the autumn of 1987. He had already produced and played on material on two albums by Dave Edmunds, and would go on to do the same for artists such as Roy Orbison, Joe Cocker, Brian Wilson, the two other remaining former Beatles, and ultimately the two 'final' Beatles tracks based on unfinished recordings left behind by John Lennon which were destined to appear on the first two 'Anthology' sets and on singles in 1995 and 1996. He released a first solo album 'Armchair Theatre' in 1990, and helped to form the Traveling Wilburys with George, Bob Dylan, Tom Petty and Roy Orbison, who released albums in 1988 and 1990 (the latter without Roy Orbison, who died shortly after the release of the first). The second of these albums featured blues guitarist Gary Moore as an honorary Wilbury on one track, and maybe it was only a missed opportunity which prevented Roy Wood from appearing in a similar role.

Roy continued to work diligently on various projects, although as he was without a record deal, a frustrating amount of material failed to find proper release. Yet at least he had the creative spark to continue recording. 'I'm happier on my own in the studio, because I know exactly what I want,' he said in 1992. 'I play a multitude of instruments so I can do it, it's much quicker than bringing a band in and more cost-effective for that matter. Unless I want a virtuoso performance on a particular instrument I'd sooner do it myself. I think you always have an urge to play live, but I don't like travelling. So as you can't do one without the other, I don't do it. If I was ever to go on the road again, I would insist on financial backing. Last time I lost money on the road.'

Was modern technology a blessing, a curse, or a two-edged sword? He admitted to being disappointed with the current state of the charts. 'It's not that I don't approve of computers in recording, as I use them myself now. But there can be a lack of feeling if you haven't got the ability to perform the songs in the traditional manner as well. For instance, I can play a cello and sample it, then play it back through a keyboard and change it as I see fit, but I have the ability to play the cello in the first place. Computers can speed things up, although I still compose on the guitar.'

Computers could be helpful, but not so record companies with an eye on the profits. 'They were saying to me, "Well, with the amount of money that we would have to spend on promoting an album of yours, we could record about a thousand of these dance records, because they're recorded in somebody's shed at the bottom of the garden on an Atari, and we know that at least a couple of hundred of them are gonna be hits." That's all they're concentrating on. My response to that was, "Well really, if you're not signing bands now that can actually play, when all this dance craze has gone out of the window, all the public are going to be left with are reissues of old Righteous Brothers records for twelve months while you get your act together", and he says, "You're right". It's one of those if-it-were-up-to-me-I'd-sign-you sort of things, because it needs to be a company decision now.' By 1990, for anybody over the age of thirty-five it was a struggle to get played on Radio 1, and as the younger people now in charge of record companies would tell everyone that, if a record was not going to get played by the station, there was not much point in releasing it.

Despite his comments about disliking travel, by 1992, going out on tour was very much part of Roy's plans once again. The catalyst for the start of a busy schedule was the press launch of the Barnardos (Midlands) Bandwagon Concert, co-organised by Bev Bevan to raise money on behalf of HIV/AIDS awareness, the homeless, and child sexual abuse victims, at Birmingham National Exhibition Centre on 7 July.

When he approached to take part in the show, Roy said yes immediately, and only then realised that he was currently bandless. With a little networking involving local Birmingham band the Poorboys who provided the rhythm section, sax player Terry Bean with whom he had worked before, and Karen Blakemore, who had played trumpet with the National Youth, Midland and Walsall Youth Jazz orchestras, a band was soon put together. Karen helped to form Thunderbirds, the all-female brass section – 'it's a dirty job, but someone's got to do it!' in his words, including fellow Walsall Orchestra players Kaye Henderson on trumpet and sisters Sue and Penny Hughes on trumpet and sax respectively. The ensemble included additional Midlands musicians, bassist Phil Tree and drummer Griff, who had both played with Mike Sheridan & the Nightriders, and keyboard player Mike Lavender, plus the Naylor twins, Sharron and Michelle, on backing vocals.

The concert at the NEC Arena on 8 October, to a capacity crowd of 7,000, was headlined by ELO Part II, with support from other acts including Tom Robinson, Ruby Turner, Edwin Starr, and the Jim Onslow Experience, led by Roy's old mate from the days of Gerry Levene and the Avengers. But it was Roy and his new 12-piece ensemble which not only stole the show but also gave the main man a new lease of life on the stage. Starting with *California Man*, a sprinkling of Wizzard and Move favourites, the latter rearranged to accommodate the brass section, and a finale of *I Wish It Could Be Christmas Everyday* with the Shrewsbury School Choir, including his nine-year-old daughter Holly, brought a rapturous reception which paralleled the one that had greeted him at his Heartbeat appearance some six years previously. It was immediately apparent that the jazz leanings of the new musicians had added an extra dimension to the songs, and in a way was a realisation of the direction that Roy had planned to explore during the latter days of Wizzard and subsequently with the Wizzo Band. Managerial politics and other factors had cut short the life of both ventures. Now, years later, it seemed as if Roy was about to have another chance to pick up where he had left off.

ELO Part II had come about largely through the efforts of Bev Bevan, and after some negotiation with Jeff, who had no wish to be involved. Several members of the previous band, some of whom had played together for a while and recorded as Orkestra, were happy to take their place in the new Jeff-less outfit, and on their first British tour in autumn 1992, Roy joined them onstage at the Bristol Colston Hall gig on 12 October for an encore of *Blackberry Way*.

As the one who had been responsible for the band's inception in the first place, it was only fitting that he should have been invited to join as a member. But although he was happy to join them on an occasional basis, that was as far as he wanted to take it, as he found it hard to take the idea seriously. 'It was like an impersonation of

ELO,' he said, 'you felt as if the ghost of Jeff was on stage.' Yet he was impressed that they had been touring with the Moscow Symphony Orchestra, an ambitious step which they had never managed to take during Jeff's leadership. ELO Part II continued until 1999, selling out live gigs around the world but unable to achieve more than fleeting chart success or overcome the prejudices of a public who saw ELO as Jeff Lynne, when Bev sold his share of the band's name back to Jeff. The latter revived the ELO name for what was probably the last time with an album 'Zoom', released in 2001 to modest sales, again featuring himself on most instruments and vocals, plus Richard Tandy on keyboards and programming, and guest appearances from Ringo Starr and the sadly terminally-ill George Harrison.

Coincidentally, this took place shortly before the time of Radio 1's 25th anniversary celebrations, with plenty of airplay for the song with which the station had started broadcasting. Carl Wayne had appeared on Terry Wogan's TV chat show as one of the musical guests, playing rhythm guitar and fronting a small band to perform *Flowers In The Rain*. It coincided with an approach he was making to Harold Wilson, by then Lord Wilson of Rievaulx, and his solicitors, requesting a reversion of the royalties to composer and performers, on the grounds that 25 years was a severe enough penalty. Sadly he was unsuccessful, and though Wilson died in 1995 there was no change in the situation, either before or since. Roy later went to court to apply for royalties to be redirected to charities of his choice, among them the Birmingham Children's Hospitals, but met with a blank refusal from the solicitors who said they were unable to change the terms. In Roy's words, it all amounted to 'a longer sentence than the train robbers'.

None of Carl's solo singles (including songs written by Roy, in addition to covers of *Miss You Nights, Deeper Than Love,* and *Imagine*, the first of many covers of the John Lennon anthem) had ever charted, and twenty years earlier he had turned down the Bickerton-Waddington song *Sugar Baby Love*, which promptly became a No. 1 hit for the Rubettes. He admitted that some of the singles he had made were 'pretty poor', especially the first, *Maybe God's Got Something Up His Sleeve*, which included 'a terrible monologue in a Birmingham voice at the beginning', and proved he would be no competition on the Las Vegas cabaret circuit for the likes of Tom Jones or Engelbert Humperdinck. But he had been very successful in other guises, including guesting on an album of Andrew Lloyd Webber songs and on Mike Oldfield's album 'Earth Moving', on several TV commercials, and onstage in musicals including Willy Russell's *Blood Brothers*. In an interview with Martin Kinch soon afterwards, he mentioned that he was probably the only former member of The Move who had remained in touch with all of them. He was full of admiration for the talents of each one, and went out of his way to speak sympathetically of Ace, with whom he had had a drink not so long before. 'I felt very sorry for him, he came from a difficult background, difficult upbringing.'

Some of the other members of Wizzard had kept in close contact. Nick, Mike and Bob had formed a jazz-rock combo, The Old Horns, to do several gigs around the Midlands area, named after a pub in Great Barr.

Early in 1993, a rejuvenated Roy, still without a record contract but well aware that public affection and the fan base were on his side, and fired with enthusiasm after having enjoyed the NEC gig so much, agreed with the other musicians that 'it was too good to just leave'. A full British tour was arranged and begun, but after four very encouraging gigs at Bristol, Yarmouth, Guildford and Swansea, and within 24 hours of the fifth date at Leicester, the promoter went bankrupt and pulled the plug, leaving Roy liable for paying the band and road crew for the tour dates they had already played. Fortunately, it was a case of being unable to keep a good man down. They managed to pick up where they had left off during the summer with various festivals, including Millwall's Lark In The Park, the International Custom Bike Show at Dymchurch, and most notably a spot alongside Fairport Convention at their annual Cropredy reunion. Although the last gig took place in August, there was no stopping them from including *I Wish It Could Be Christmas Everyday* in the set, complete with fake snow onstage and a Santa Claus tossing crackers to the audience.

However, he was adamant that there was no question of reviving The Move or Wizzard, despite what promoters and others might tell him to the contrary. 'I'd rather pack up before I have to do that. I want this to be a new thing, but obviously, the people who pay money to see us expect us to play the stuff they know. I'm not ashamed to play it, because I wrote it, but I would like to present it in a different way, so people don't say, "Oh, he's just doing it like Wizzard or The Move". Part of the reason why I did change the arrangements is so that I just wasn't playing the same old thing I used to play years ago. I need to keep my own interest going as well. We've got the brass section playing all those riffs in *I Can Hear The Grass Grow*, and *Fire Brigade*, with the reggae horns.'

The weeks leading up to Christmas 1993 saw a short English tour which included venues at Leicester (where they had been due to play that spring), Preston, Plymouth, Folkestone, Northampton, Hemel Hempstead, and appropriately at Birmingham NEC. A set comprising rearrangements of tried and trusted old favourites, plus *1-2-3*, included four new compositions, namely *Kiss Me Goodnight Boadicea, House Of Love, Lion's Heart,* and *Electric Age.* In a newspaper Q & A around this time, when Roy was asked who was his most admired historical figure, he named Boadicea; 'she was pretty weird, and we have the same hairstyle!' He stressed that there was a wonderful atmosphere with the new band. 'Everyone's got a good sense of humour. It's great. I just look forward to it every time. You can't have a day with them and not have a good laugh. I even enjoy rehearsals now. Previously, getting me to rehearsals was like pulling teeth! Now I really enjoy it because we're creating something fresh and new.' If he didn't enjoy playing with these people, he emphasised, he wouldn't be doing it any more. As various members had to pull out and news ones took their place, they all fitted in and became one of the gang in no time. They had all reached the point 'where we know each other well enough to be able to have a bit of a laugh, and take the piss out of each other, basically. The brass girls are the worst for that!'

Once again the jinx struck just hours before what was to have been the third date at Oldham on 5 December. When they stopped off for a meal on their way, much of their gear was stolen from the tour bus. Three guitars, one of which was Roy's 1958 red Fender of great sentimental value, radio mikes, keyboards, a trumpet, trombones and tenor saxes all went missing. At the venue a distraught Roy waited in the foyer to chat, sign autographs and apologise personally to disappointed ticket holders, as he assured them that the gig would be rescheduled for January. New equipment and instruments were borrowed, hired or replaced for the next performance on the tour four days later.

On 22 December, a few hours prior to the Hemel Hempstead gig, the band went to the BBC Maida Vale Studios where they played a live session on the Radio 1 lunchtime show, introduced by Jakki Brambles and attended by Carl and his son Jack. Ironically, this was only a few weeks after the notorious shakeout in which the station's new controller had axed most of the long-serving DJs, and effectively banned the vast majority of any music which was not considered 'new'. Three old favourites, namely *See My Baby Jive, Blackberry Way*, and *Christmas Everyday*, were performed alongside *Kiss Me Goodnight Boadicea* and *House Of Love*. After such exposure, and hot on the heels of a very well-received tour on which the new material had proved that the songwriting genius had never faded, the time was right for a new record deal. There was material for a new single, with talk of a new studio album provisionally called 'Electric Age', and a live set, 'Alive'.

Frustratingly, neither ever happened, although there were no doubts about the quality of the new songs. In December 1994 Roy appeared on Chris Evans' *Don't Forget Your Toothbrush*, in a spot which included him competing with superfan Martin Kinch on 'questions about Roy Wood' (Martin won, walking off with a pair of Roy's glasses as a reward), and performing *Kiss Me Goodnight Boadicea* with Jools Holland and his Big Band. Jools took the vocal on the second verse of the song, and the performance had all the audience standing up dancing in their seats at once. It was a tailor-made opportunity for a new, eagerly-awaited release if ever there was one.

Though fans would wait in vain for another record featuring nothing but new songs, yet short British tours by Roy and his band were becoming a more or less annual fixture. That same year saw them taking to the road, including appearances with them onstage from Kim Wilde (who contributed a glorious version of the Fontella Bass oldie *Rescue Me*) and anarchic fiddle virtuoso Nigel Kennedy, whom Roy had long admired. Roy was now managing himself and the band. 'I've been mismanaged enough in the past. I can't mismanage myself any worse, can I really? I might as well have a go. Plus, I don't have to pay 25% to some tosser who doesn't really know what he's doing. In the past, I've never been what you'd call a good businessman. I haven't got that sort of brain. But I'm getting more into the swing of being able to negotiate with people, which is what it's all about, really.'

1995 proved a veritable feast in more ways than one. The BBC had commissioned and screened a series of documentary programmes on TV based around Pete Frame's exemplary book of rock family trees, and needless to say, the intricacies of the Birmingham rock scene were an obvious choice for one of the first programmes. The labyrinthine connections between The Move, Wizzard, ELO, the Moody Blues and several of the earlier acts were explored alongside a selection on film clips and interview soundbites from Roy and the other leading personnel. Over on Channel 4, a programme on the top ten glam rock acts was served up, with Slade not surprisingly topping the selection, but Wizzard pitching in cheerfully at No. 7. Roy was interviewed, talking about the records and also discussing the fact that the first British acts to wear face paint in that style were him and – even before him – Arthur Brown, whose appearance on *Top Of The Pops* fronting The Crazy World of Arthur Brown on their one and only hit, the chart-topping *Fire* in the summer of 1968, had truly seemed like a vision from another planet.

In August, the band made a second appearance at the Cropredy Festival with Fairport Convention. An extraordinary combination of talent was seen onstage when Roy and his band joined forces with Richard Thompson. The set included *California Man, Fire Brigade, Blackberry Way* and *Are You Ready To Rock* (a song now increasingly referred to, especially on set lists used onstage, in its abbreviated phonetic spelling, *RU Red E 2 Rock*), interspersed with a handful of Richard's songs like *I Want To See the Bright Lights Tonight*, and *Tear Stained Letter*, with Roy and Richard taking lead vocals on their own respective numbers. One recording from the proceedings, the old Motown classic *I Heard It Through The Grapevine*, with Richard on vocal and brass arranged by Roy, was released in 1997 on a Fairport Convention CD on their own label Woodworm Records, 'Who Knows Where the Time Goes'.

A new ostensibly live recording, apparently doctored according to regular practice in the studio, of *I Wish It Could Be Christmas Everyday*, appeared on a four-track CD single on the Woody label in December 1995. With a soundcheck version of the same song, plus *Santa Claus Is Coming To Town*, featuring backing vocalists Sharon and Michelle Naylor on lead vocals, and a demo version of *Lion's Heart*, it registered in the charts at No. 59 in a two-week run.

By the time he reached his fifties, Roy had attained genuine celebrity status and was rapidly becoming a fairly familiar face on various TV shows. He appeared on comedy music quiz show *Never Mind The Buzzcocks* one week as part of regular captain Phill Jupitus' team, on *This Is Your Life* as a guest on an edition featuring Suzi Quatro (whose debut hit, *Can The Can*, had knocked *See My Baby Jive* off the top spot in June 1973), and on *Can't Cook, Won't Cook*, a celebrity 'cooking' show in which he and Kelly Groucutt of ELO and ELO Part II and their daughters Holly and Jenny went head to head, or rather pan to pan. Kelly's culinary efforts were judged the better of the two.

When not playing with his own band, Roy made occasional appearances with others. From time to time he was seen on stage as a member of the S.A.S. Band, alias Spikey's All Stars, a loose conglomeration of hitmakers including among others Leo Sayer, Graham Gouldman, Tony Hadley, Tom Robinson, both Paul Youngs (the solo singer of *Wherever I Lay My Hat* fame, and the lead vocalist of Sad Cafe and Mike & the Mechanics, who died suddenly in 2000), assembled and led by Spike Edney, who had been Queen's keyboard player on live dates and then an integral part of the band formed by Brian May after Freddie Mercury's death. When Cheap Trick played Rock City at Nottingham, Roy and daughter Holly went along for the show, and Roy went onstage to do a few of his and their songs with them, before being brought back on for the encore to play on *I Want You To Want Me* and *Dream Police*.

As one of Birmingham's favourite musical sons, it was only appropriate that Roy should be called upon to take a major hand in the celebrations for Millennium Night in the city's Centenary Square. Timing being all important on such an occasion, not least for a live broadcast by the BBC, Roy and the band played a half-hour set of favourites, opening as ever with California Man and finishing with *Christmas Everyday,* before Sir Cliff Richard led a countdown at midnight from the stage and Roy sprayed the band with champagne. Appropriate merrymaking followed in the nearest hotel bar, after which somebody was noticed furtively trying without success to unlock his room door by inserting his credit card into the slot as he had mislaid his hotel card.

Over the years, various recordings which had long been shelved or even considered lost were coming to light. The whereabouts of the unreleased 1976 Wizzard album had been one of rock music's great mysteries, but over twenty years later they were found when staff at Demon/Westside Records, who were examining material from the vaults of Trojan, the label which had taken over the back catalogue formerly owned by Jet, discovered the master tapes to a set of songs they did not recognise. The trail led them back to Roy, and at last it was released in March 2000 by Edsel Records, who had previously reissued *Introducing Eddy And The Falcons* and *Mustard* on CD, both with bonus tracks.

Named 'Main Street' after the opening track, to reflect some of Roy's influences at the time of recording the album derived from time spent in the city, it consisted of eight tracks. Three of them, namely the 1979 B-side *Saxmaniax*, the Wizzo Band-premiered *French Perfume*, and the single *Indiana Rainbow,* had already received some exposure. For the most part, it was a sophisticated fusion of rock and jazz which had some critics making comparisons with latter-period Steely Dan, some distance removed from the hit single-orientated outfit of 1973 and the rock'n'roll band of the following year. The acoustic guitar of *French Perfume* clearly revealed a Django Reinhardt influence, while the longest track, at over seven minutes, *The Fire In His Guitar*, was driven partly by an electric guitar figure which recalled the early work of Hendrix. The credits named a six-piece Wizzard, with Rick on bass and pedal steel guitars, Mike and Nick on saxes and flutes, Bob on piano, and Charlie on drums, congas and percussion as well as guest vocals on *Don't You Feel Better*.

A note in the booklet by Roy himself referred to 'the powers that be (at the time) [who] decided in their infinite wisdom that this album should not be released....In my opinion, this was nothing short of a crime.' It was 'probably a last attempt to retain some sort of sanity, trying to grow up, and not carry on indefinitely being just another pop group.' Had it been released when first created, he believed, his writing style would have taken a different curve, and the band would have then been performing the type of material that bands such as Jamiroquai were having at the time that it finally saw the light of day.

Another new single with considerable input from Roy appeared that Christmas. However, far from offering anything new, it turned out to be a collaboration with Mike Batt, *I Wish It Could Be A Wombling Merry Christmas Everyday*. Mike, who like Roy had recently been made a member of the Society of Distinguished Songwriters, had originally suggested the idea to Roy, and it all took shape over a couple of drinks. Credited to the Wombles with Roy Wood, with a little help from the string section of the Royal Philharmonic Orchestra, and released on Mike's Dramatico label, it was also used in part as promotion for a new Wombles CD, with a press launch in November at the Langham Hilton Hotel, London, at which both songwriters appeared with Orinoco, Uncle Bulgaria and the rest. The furry creatures had come close to capturing the festive bullseye in December 1974 with *Wombling Merry Christmas,* a bouncy sax-driven song that wore its Wizzard influences boldly on its sleeve, only held at bay by yet another offering that year in similar mode, Mud's Elvis spoof *Lonely This Christmas*. Aired during the crucial pre-Christmas week on television by the BBC on *Top Of The Pops 2* and various other TV shows, it went one week better than Roy's 1984 chart re-appearance, entering at its peak position of No. 22. Yet there must have been many a fan who thought it was nothing short of a butchery of both songs. In their view, the effort would have been far better expended in releasing a single, if not an album, containing some of the as yet unreleased material which had been appearing in the live act for several years.

Roy was also busy on the radio around this time. One day he deputised for broadcaster Ed Doolan, presenter of a weekday show broadcast on the 9-12 a.m. slot each weekday on Radio WM. As it was a consumer programme in which listeners might ring in asking for advice on what to do about leaking patio doors and the like, he had gleefully looked forward to giving out a little misinformation in the interests of making a laugh and causing the odd little bit of chaos, although one might think that punters tuning in to the show would know better than to regard him as the fount of all knowledge on DIY. Instead the producers, perhaps wisely, chose to let their star presenter focus on music and interviewing various guests instead. Among them were Dr Bernard Trafford, headmaster of Wolverhampton Grammar School, John Hughes, director of the Walsall Jazz Orchestra, former Beatles' press officer Tony Barrow,

Mike Batt, and Carl Wayne. A few months later he was one of the guests on Ken Bruce's regular 'Tracks Of My Years' feature on the BBC Radio 2 morning show, choosing ten favourite pieces of music and commenting on them. Among his choices were ZZ Top's *Legs*, Elvis Presley's *Jailhouse Rock*, Gary Moore's *Parisian Walkways*, a movement from Vivaldi's *The Four Seasons* played by Nigel Kennedy, Led Zeppelin's *Whole Lotta Love*, and Stevie Wonder's *Superstition*.

Foremost among his various TV appearances was one on Carlton TV, shown in the Midlands in January 2002. Introduced by Noddy Holder, it included a preview of a new Big Band song, *Spektacular* [sic], written and performed in salsa style. This was accompanied by a short interview in which Roy commented on the ageist outlook of most radio programmes, increasingly reluctant to play new material by any performer over thirty-five, and said that it would probably be released under a different name altogether, the MDO or Mega Dance Orquestra. As in the case of other post-1990 material, fans are still awaiting its release.

Since the last two or three years of the twentieth century, with CD purchasers becoming ever more demanding and with the constant quest for more historical recordings being unearthed from the vaults, Roy's earlier back catalogue would benefit handsomely. The first of major significance was 'Movements: 30th Anniversary Anthology', a 3-CD boxed set released by Westside Records in 1997, containing 54 tracks. In addition to the entire Move catalogue up to the end of 1970, it included a few rough mixes and alternate versions, such as an early undubbed *Fire Brigade* minus the additional vocals and sound effects, an Italian language *Something*, additional live tracks from the Marquee in 1968 not used on the 'Something Else' EP, and the first legitimate release of the B-side that never was, *Vote For Me*. From then on, a brace of Move compilations would feature the latter track.

Remastered versions of the old albums, plus bonus tracks, out-takes, live recordings and radio sessions appeared on carefully-packaged reissues (containing written contributions by some of the original creators) of the Harvest Move, ELO and Roy Wood solo albums on EMI from 2001 onwards. 'Wizzard Brew' appeared in 2006 at around the time of Roy's sixtieth birthday, expanded with the inclusion of both sides of all four Harvest singles (and notes by the present author in the accompanying booklet). An original plan to include a bonus CD consisting of previously unreleased Wizzard studio material, out-takes and early live recordings, 'Off To See The Wizzard', was shelved, but a limited number of test pressings was issued for limited circulation. One such CD was auctioned on eBay in 2012 and attracted a winning bid of £206.

A CD of sessions recorded for the BBC, which appeared in 1998, included alternate recordings of some of the early hits alongside *Stop! Get A Hold Of Myself*, *Morning Dew*, *California Girls* and *Kentucky Woman*, was the successor to a widely-circulated bootleg, 'Black Country Rock'. Among the compilations 'Exotic Mixture: Singles A's & B's' on the German Repertoire label in 1999 stood out, gathering as it did 39 tracks on two CDs from his solo career from 1972 to 1987 and from several different labels, including the increasingly hard-to-obtain singles recorded with The Wizzo Band, Annie Haslam, and the Rockers – even if it misspelt the B-side of *Oh What A Shame* as *Bengal Jim*. Even better was Sanctuary Records' 'Look Thru' The Eyes Of Roy Wood & Wizzard: Hits & Rarities 1974-87'. Again a double CD, its 30 tracks included some alternative mixes and takes of material familiar to fans, plus the bonuses of several previously unreleased gems, such as a jingle recorded for Kenny Everett's Capital Radio show in May 1975, four live tracks recorded by Wizzard on their autumn 1974 US tour, and *Human Cannonball*, a cut from the band's final sessions which had been omitted from 'Main Street'.

Alongside these, inevitably, were some rather shoddy, poorly-planned compilations. 'I wish these companies would actually liaise with me a bit more – at all, in fact,' he said ruefully. 'It's still my face on the front. So really, I should have some sort of say as to what tracks go on there, and which order they go in. Because the problem with compilation albums in the past is that they put a few hits on there, and then they pad it out with sort of strange album tracks.' The only one which had been any good in his view was the double vinyl 'The Roy Wood Story' released on Harvest in 1976 - but even that one 'could have been better'.

Just as eagerly awaited was a phased definitive release of The Move's back catalogue to the end of 1970 on Salvo during 2007 and 2008. 'Move', 'Shazam' and 'Looking On' all appeared with bonus tracks and out-takes, each one accompanied by painstakingly researched and assembled booklets which covered all the original releases on Regal Zonophone and Fly. It culminated in what was a dream come true for many fans in 2008, a four-CD collection 'Anthology'. Spanning The Move's entire career from the initial pre-Deram recordings in 1966 to their farewell offerings for Harvest six years later, it included previously unissued live material, alternative takes such as *Fire Brigade* with Matthew Fisher on piano, *Simple Simon* which would never be taken any further, and two rough demos of *Second Class*, with Roy on acoustic guitar and Trevor on drums, a song which later emerged as *She's Too Good For Me* on 'Boulders'.

Sadly the original vocalist was no longer around to see the final result. Carl Wayne's career had in a sense come full circle in 2000 when he took over lead vocals in another band who had enjoyed consistent success in the 1960s, The Hollies, replacing Allan Clarke who was retiring for various reasons. They undertook extensive tours at home and overseas, and on live dates playing old Hollies and Move songs, including *Flowers In The Rain* and *Blackberry Way*. Also a regular on the set list was Mud's 1974 chart-topping *Tiger Feet*, a nod to bassist Ray Stiles, who had been a member of the band at the time and joined the Hollies in 1988. Carl had gone into hospital for a check-up shortly after completing a tour with the band, but died of cancer of the oesophagus in August 2004, aged 61.

A fitting tribute to the singer would come with the release of 'Songs From The Wood And Beyond, 1973-2003', a CD of tracks by Carl Wayne recorded over a thirty-year span and released by Sanctuary in 2006. Five of them were compositions by Roy, including both sides of the 1982 single *Aerial Pictures* and *Colourful Lady*, alongside the previously unissued *Givin' Your Heart Away*, *Hazel Eyes* and *Hot Cars*. Roy produced all five, in addition to editing and remastering the whole collection, and penning an affectionate note to salute the memory of 'a larger than life character' who was sadly missed.

Roy was highly displeased when Bev formed a band billed in some instances as Bev Bevan's Move, or even just The Move, playing some of the old material. The line-up included Trevor Burton on guitar and vocals – ironically, given the latter's acrimonious departure in 1969 after a clash with Bev onstage –

alongside, at various times, former ELO Part II guitarists Phil Bates and Neil Lockwood. Roy dismissed the outfit as 'The Imposter Move Motherf**kers'. He issued a statement emphasising that Bev did not have his permission to do so, and he intended to oppose it at every opportunity. 'Imagine Ringo Starr going on the road as "The Beatles"?' Those who bought tickets to see the band were duly warned in good faith not to expect to see him among the line-up of what was in his view basically nothing more than a tribute group.

Bev and Trevor were quick to put their side of the argument on their website. They pointed out that Roy had been invited to take part in the venture on more than one occasion and had declined. 'His brilliance as a songwriter and his contribution to the band are acknowledged at every show,' they acknowledged. 'It seems such a shame that the same professional courtesy is not afforded to us in return. We would much prefer to deal with any issues Roy may have face to face rather than through the media but we did not make that choice. Roy knows very well, our door remains open any time he wants to talk.' The 21st century Move, which in its final line-up included Phil Tree on bass, Tony Kelsey on guitar and Abby Brant on keyboards, in addition to Bev and Trevor, with all sharing vocals, called it a day in 2014. Early that year Bev announced online that, owing to members' other commitments with their own bands in future, their final show would be at the Weyfest, Farnham, on 30 August. Prior to that they played a full gig sheet, including an appearance onstage at the Isle of Wight Festival in June.

Coincidentally, this happened at the same time that some media interest had been created, with several interviews in the national press and on the radio, to celebrate the reissuing and remastering of 'Boulders' in the summer of 2007. In the accompanying booklet, he mentioned the delays which had held up its release in the first place (although his statement that it had been finished and ready for release in 1969 was not borne out by earlier interviews and studio logs), and his motivation for recording a solo album on which he could play every instrument, sing all the vocals, produce and mix all the tracks, paint the album sleeve, drive the van and make the tea.

Why the title 'Boulders'? He might have called it 'Bollocks', he said, if he had been allowed to, but in 1973 – four years before the Sex Pistols 'Never Mind The Bollocks' controversy - EMI (or any major label, for that matter) would almost certainly have said no. Talking to Adam Sweeting of the *Daily Telegraph*, he spoke about his love of the album, on the ongoing Bev and Move situation, and briefly on Don Arden, who had died in July at the age of 81 after a long battle with Alzheimer's Disease. Saying wryly that he seemed to have mislaid the number for Interflora, Roy was too honest to utter any mealy-mouthed sentiments about the man whom he said had ruined his career. In his view, Arden was 'a crooked manager who couldn't keep his fingers out of the till', had deliberately fermented animosity between him and Jeff Lynne in the summer of 1972 in order to induce one of them to walk away from ELO and form another money-spinning outfit which would provide yet another source of income for the Arden empire, and he, Roy, had as much chance of becoming Lord Mayor of London as of getting his money back from him.

Don saw it differently. Roy, he had remarked in his autobiography, was a tremendous musician who wrote incredible songs 'but he let himself drift off into fantasy land' and stopped being a star virtually overnight. 'He should have been the biggest star in the world', the manager maintained, but he destroyed his chances as he would not listen, or did not care, or was maybe even scared of it.

Over the years ELO had staunchly defended Arden's record as their manager and the man whose wholehearted backing had been a major part of their success, but other acts who had formerly been his clients, notably surviving members of the Small Faces and Lynsey de Paul, were like Roy less charitable. The Ardens' reputation had certainly not been helped by a consumers' BBC radio programme, *Checkpoint*, in 1979, in which researcher and presenter Roger Cook had exposed some of Don's less savoury managerial dealings and left him incandescent with rage, unable to mount a coherent defence of his methods. In the mid-1980s the press was full of tales of Don's former business partner at Jet Records being kidnapped, physically attacked and accused of misappropriating company funds. David Arden served a prison sentence after being found guilty for his role in the episode, while Don was later placed on trial but acquitted of all charges. Nevertheless the family's good name, such as it was, never really recovered from the incident.

On a happier note, the charts at around this time continued to confirm that *I Wish It Could Be Christmas Everyday* was one of everybody's favourite festive oldies. The record regularly became part of radio station playlists at the end of each year, and Roy promoted it on various TV programmes, among them as a guest on chat shows hosted by Terry Wogan and Jonathan Ross, and on comedy show *The Kumars At No. 42*.

After the singles and album chart compilation rules were altered to take account of download sales as well as those of physical copies, in December 2007 the Top 75 was notable for a large influx of tinsel tunes which had not charted for some years, or in one or two cases never even issued as singles before. Boosted partly after its use in an Argos advertisement on TV in which he starred as a rowdy neighbour irritating the hell out of those living within earshot, *I Wish It Could Be Christmas Everyday* peaked that month at No. 16 – his highest singles chart placing since *Oh What A Shame* had made No. 13 thirty-two years earlier. It looked set to become a regular if not annual chart re-entry, returning in December 2008 to peak at No. 31, then 2009 (No. 45), 2010 (No. 46), 2011 (No. 28), 2012 (No. 29), and 2013 (No. 31). By December 2013 it had clocked up over forty weeks on the singles chart altogether, if the original 1973 release, and the 1981 and 1984 reissues were added to the 2007 and onwards download totals, plus an additional two weeks if the Big Band 1995 re-recording was included. On most of those years it hit a higher position than its fellow re-entrant from Slade, a feat which gave its creator no little satisfaction.

The honours for the record were not over by any means. In 2010, a Phonographic Performance Ltd survey of the most-played festive songs in shops and on radio during the past decade placed the Wizzard song at No. 5, beaten only by its competitors from Mariah Carey at No. 1, followed by Wham!, the Pogues with Kirsty MacColl, and Slade in that order. Yet while royalties from the record contributed to his pension, whenever it came on the radio he switched it off, and he even avoided Yuletide shopping trips in the city centre in order to avoid not having to hear it constantly in-store. He was looking forward to going to one of his favourite pubs on Christmas Day, he said, adding that it would be lovely 'as long as that song doesn't come on.' Some years earlier, he had commented, 'Everyone thinks I just curled up and died after making that record!'

However, the record's enduring success might be considered some compensation for the fact that *Flowers In The Rain* has also been among his most frequently-aired oldies on the radio over the years, yet thanks to Secunda's shenanigans was fated never to earn him a penny in royalties.

It even had the dubious distinction of being covered on festive CDs by the likes of the Spice Girls, Girls Aloud and The Wurzels. Arguably worse, it was also named by Dr George Rae, a Tyneside practitioner, as being partly responsible for a seasonal outbreak of capsulitis. Middle-aged people, he said, who did not dance at any other time of year, tended to turn up at surgeries around Christmas time suffering from 'glam rock shoulder' or frozen shoulders, a form of repetitive stress injury, apparently caused by punching the air at parties when certain records were playing. The main culprits named for causing this complaint were *I Wish It Could Be Christmas Everyday* and Jeff Beck's *Hi Ho Silver Lining*.

On 18 January 2008, Roy found himself donning an academic gown and hood and taking a seat in the main hall at the University of Derby, where he was created an Honorary Doctor of Music in recognition of his work as an international performing musician and creative figure in British music. After accepting his honour from the academic staff, and commenting to laughter that he was not the only person who enjoyed dressing up and that being there felt 'like being on stage with the D'Oyly Carte Opera Company', in his address of thanks he said that he had been in the music business for more years than he cared to remember, but he had never received an honour which meant more to him than this one did. It would certainly spur him, he assured his audience, on to further composing work. The world still awaits the premiere of this.

Another honour followed on 10 June 2010, when he was presented with a Mojo Classic Songwriter Award. *Mojo* editor-in-chief Phil Alexander said in his citation that Roy had not only formed three classic British bands, but had also written some of the best pop music of any era, 'all before he'd turned 22', and influenced everyone from Paul Weller to Kiss.

On 13 November 2010, a long-running campaign by the Midlands newspaper *Sunday Mercury* to 'make Woody a star' came to fruition, when he followed in the tradition of other local celebrities including Noddy Holder, Chris Tarrant, Murray Walker and Lenny Henry in taking his place on the Birmingham Walk of Stars at Broad Street. After being pulled through the city streets in a reindeer-drawn sleigh, and switching on the Christmas lights, he was presented with the honour by the Lord Mayor of Birmingham. However, various delays resulted in the star not being cemented in until a year later, and within a few days the stone had cracked badly on one corner due to a fault in the materials used. Although it was reported immediately, the Broad Street Business Improvement District said that in order to save on costs, it could not be repaired until another two stars were added. The stones were so heavy that special machinery was required to lift them.

During the preceding months, Roy had turned to journalism, writing occasional guest columns for the local press. These commented on such issues as the proposed introduction of identity cards, which he condemned as unnecessary and excessively expensive legislation, binge drinking and the folly of extending licensing hours, and the abysmal quality of daytime television, with genuine entertainment on the small screen having seemingly become the product of a bygone era.

To the casual observer too young to remember the late 1960s and early 1970s, it sometimes seemed as if Roy was in danger of being remembered for one record in particular, particularly when Christmas came round and he could be relied upon to appear on TV promoting 'that song' yet again. A few comments on internet sites even suggested that the record had been a millstone around his neck, and overshadowed if not even destroyed his career.

Yet there were those happy to look beyond it and accord him rightful recognition for the considerable body of work he had done over several years. In April 2009 Radio 2 broadcast a documentary in its occasional series *The Record Producers*, in which presenter Richard Allinson and fellow producer Steve Levine interviewed him and others and examined the original multi-tracks of some of his recordings in minute detail, revealing the extraordinarily complex work and meticulous planning which had gone into recording the backing tracks for songs such as *10538 Overture, Angel Fingers* and *Forever*. The analysis of *Angel Fingers*, for example, demonstrated the way that Roy had built up the huge wall of sound which included three bass guitars, three drums, two pianos double-tracked (in other words, four pianos), and up to twenty saxophones. An expanded edition of the programme was also broadcast on the sister radio channel BBC6.

Later that year Roy was credited as co-writer of a new Christmas record released for charity. *My Christmas Card To You*, credited to Shooting Stars, was penned jointly by him, DJ Mike Read, and new singer-songwriter Elliott Frisby, though it was transparently based in part on the tune to *Angel Fingers*. All the profits were to go to the Shooting Star Children's Hospice. Despite a video which featured Read prominently alongside his former Radio 1 colleague David Hamilton and Dave Hill of Slade, the record received scant publicity and never charted.

Meanwhile the Roy Wood Big Band, The Roy Wood Army, or The Roy Wood Temporarily Not So Big Band, under whatever name, continued to take to the road towards the end of each year. A tour which saw them supporting Status Quo on several dates on their pre-Christmas jaunt in 2009 recruited many new fans. Some of them could have been forgiven for wondering where he had been the last few years, while others were too young to remember him from first time round, as they came along with their mums and dads primarily to see the band who had by then clocked up more hits on the UK chart than any other. In a press conference to announce the tour, Quo front man Francis Rossi, who had recently divested himself of the most famous ponytail in rock, quipped that he would be 'the one with the newly short hair'.

A few new tracks by Roy and the band had leaked into the media through various outlets, as fans continued to wait for their eventual legitimate release. These included *Kiss Me Goodnight Boadicea*, a stage favourite ever since his early nineties return to live music, *Big Girl Blues*, with shared female lead vocals, and the instrumental *Roy's Revenge*, which with its heavy use of the brass section and also a drum solo, harked back to the more experimental days of the Wizzo Band, although this time it was kept to a more concise four minutes or so.

In the autumn of 2011 Status Quo announced dates for their Quofest, an eleven-date British tour in December with Roy and his band and also Kim Wilde supporting as they played venues including the London 0$_2$, Birmingham LG, Sheffield Motorpoint and Liverpool Echo Arenas, Glasgow SECC, Brighton Centre, and Plymouth Pavilions. At the gigs, fans would be rewarded not merely by seeing separate sets from all three acts, but also a cheerily rough-and-ready performance at the end of old festive favourites like *Winter Wonderland* and *Santa Claus Is Coming To Town*, with Roy and Francis Rossi trading different verses.

Unhappily, Roy was grappling with a new problem at this point. Several months of back problems were forcing him to spend increasing amounts of time sitting down, even on stage. Two slipped discs and stenosis, a narrowing of the spinal canal, were making him feel like he had electric shocks going down his legs, and standing for long periods of time was sheer agony. While years of energetic performance on stage with a heavy guitar around his neck, and more recently an accident in which his 4x4 overturned, had undoubtedly contributed, he blamed it largely on too much time spent in front of a computer, and bending over controls in the studio; 'You can get carried away and be in there for hours.'

The dates coincided with the release in November 2011 by EMI, on the Harvest label, of 'Music Book', a 36-track double CD which featured songs from all phases of Roy's career and from several different labels, largely remastered old recordings from The Move, ELO, and Wizzard days as well as a handful of solo material. There were however two recordings by Roy and the new band (only two, tantalisingly for fans who could have been forgiven for expecting maybe four times as many), including the new song *New York City* and a live version of the perennial show-opener, the rearranged *California Man*, alongside a completely re-recorded solo version of *Fire Brigade*, 'in the shed', and a new recording of *Blackberry Way* with an additional string intro. There were also two of his songs as covered by others, Status Quo's *I Can Hear the Grass Gro*w and Nancy Sinatra's *Flowers In the Rain*. Compiled and edited by Roy with Dick Plant, the package was dedicated to Holly, 'my daughter and best friend', and to the memory of Carl Wayne. The booklet contained a generous selection of photos from the archives over the years, from one of a fair-haired little Roy of some three years of age, to another of Roy and his longtime hero Jimmy Page together clutching their awards at a *Mojo* honours ceremony in 2010.

Early in 2012, Roy revealed that he was considering leaving not only his Derbyshire home, but indeed England, to go and start a new life in New York. Holly was about to marry and planned to move to New York in order to be closer to her mother Sam, from whom Roy had been divorced for several years. He said he would see how she got on in the big apple, and then perhaps he would go and live there himself.

From time to time there would be occasional appearances in the news. A Coventry newspaper reported rather acidly in November 2012 that council staff who were being made redundant as a result of cuts in public spending would be less than delighted to know that the Christmas lights were to be switched on by Roy that year. For flicking a switch and singing a special version of his festive hit, wrote the paper, he was being paid £7,000.

There had been no Roy Wood Christmas tour that year. However his programme for the winter months of 2013 was scheduled to include an interview onstage at Birmingham Town Hall with friend and television presenter Nick Owen, discussing his life and times in music, followed by a performance with the band at Symphony Hall for a fortieth anniversary celebration of the Christmas hit. Earlier that year, in July, he had headlined a benefit gig for Mike Burney, who had been unable to work while undergoing treatment for cancer, the disease which would ultimately claim his life in November 2014. As part of the 2013 Birmingham International Jazz & Blues Festival, Roy and his band topped a bill which also featured The Steve Gibbons Band and King Pleasure & the Biscuit Boys, and raised over £3,000.

These shows featured a rejuvenated Roy Wood, who in the summer of 2012 had undergone five hours of surgery in hospital to ease the back problems. Two surgeons carefully repaired three discs and shaved part of his spine away in a successful procedure to restore his failing mobility. The condition, he revealed, had had a major impact on his life, preventing him from doing many of the things he wanted to do.

'It was so frustrating,' he admitted. 'I did a few gigs but I couldn't stand up on stage all the way through them. I had to sit on a high stool – and that just meant more problems. A lot of my songs are hard to sing and you simply cannot sing them sitting down because you can't hit the high notes properly. When you're sitting down you can't take the deep breath you need, and your diaphragm is restricted. Even Pavarotti would have found it difficult.' The surgeons, he added, did an absolutely brilliant job and he could not thank them enough.

In March 2014 Roy and Jeff were reunited for the first time in twenty years or so when the latter was honoured on the Broad Street Walk of Stars at Birmingham. The local press readily reported that the meeting began with a handshake, and an awkward hug, before the memories flowed and they caught up on each others' news, not least the fact that Roy had just become a grandfather with the birth of Holly's baby son. Afterwards both readily paid tribute to the other as well as testifying how good it was to meet up with old friends from days gone by, especially Richard Tandy, the former ELO keyboard player whose active association with The Move stretched back as far as the days when Carl Wayne fronted the band. Inevitably there was speculation that both the Brum musical giants might work together again, even if only to collaborate on another song or two. Had they both moved on? Time would tell – maybe.

In the summer Roy was seen appearing alongside long-time friend Rick Wakeman on the TV game show *Pointless*, on which they comprised the winning team. A further, greater honour came in September when Rick, as King Rat of The Grand Order of Water Rats, presided over the induction of Roy into the organisation. He was impressed and amused at how old-fashioned the ceremony was, as the same wording was used as when the Order was founded in 1889. Actor Frazer Hines of Dr Who fame led him blindfolded into the ceremonial room, and comedian Roy Hudd wrote a special poem for him which he recited at the ceremony and signed for him. At the same time he was invited to play at the 125th Anniversary Gala Ball in London, together with a full orchestra and The English Chamber Choir. 'Today Roy Wood becomes a Water Rat,' Rick tweeted. 'All the "Rats" are thrilled. It'll be Christmas Every Day & we'll celebrate with Blackberry Way Pie.'

8. ...and finally

Roy Wood – is he one of the most talented, imaginative performers, composers and producers in British rock? Or, as some reference books and critics might suggest, is he merely an inspired craftsman with an inexhaustible knack for re-creating others' styles but unable to create his own?

In the early days of rock'n'roll, Eddie Cochran would lay down all guitars, bass, drums and vocals in the recording studio. Following the example of one of his earliest idols, Roy was one of the first British performers to make extensive use of multi-tracking and overdubbing facilities for all voices and instruments, and he was without doubt an influence on such mid-1970s epic singles as *I'm Not In Love* and *Bohemian Rhapsody*, on which heavily-overdubbed vocals by 10cc and Queen respectively were such a vital component. However, as often as not, Roy's recordings also included brass, woodwind and string arrangements, and after the first Move album he not only played most of the instruments but also produced the results, as well as writing much of the words and music. This might be compared with the comparatively limited studio achievements of the Beatles, whose more sophisticated recordings owed as much to the production, arrangements and imagination of George Martin and later on Phil Spector as to their own efforts, and who used additional session musicians as a matter of course. This is in no way intended to diminish the Fab Four's abilities, for three of them were accomplished multi-instrumentalists themselves, and Paul McCartney, the most musically gifted of all, would give ample proof on his first solo album 'McCartney' in 1970, which was effectively his 'Boulders'. During their early years the Rolling Stones also had their own Roy Wood-like figure in Brian Jones, who could play more or less any instrument at will, but Jones' lack of staying power, unrealised potential and ultimate fate is of course one of the saddest stories in rock music.

One-man band units would become commonplace enough in the 1980s, but with the advent of computers there was a world of difference between programming Linn drums, synthesisers and voice processors as they did, and overdubbing guitars, conventional drums, saxes, bassoons, cellos, bagpipes, oboe, and clarinet, not to mention multi-tracked choral vocals, as had been pioneered by Roy in the days of 16-track technology, from 'Boulders' onwards. The only similar British figure in the early 1970s who played and sang almost everything in the studio was Dave Edmunds, another Phil Spector admirer – and when it came to songs, Dave was always better known for cover versions than for writing his own material.

Admittedly, Roy never had a silver or gold LP, and he never managed to repeat his British chart success in the US. Maybe has been too eager sometimes to move on, rather than hit on a winning formula, play safe and stick with it until fans lose interest, a charge that could perhaps be levelled at too many a hit-making machine from the last forty years or so. But his reputation in the British rock scene is almost unrivalled, and his achievements over the years have left many of his peers standing.

As the various awards of recent years recognise, his place rests on foundations considerably more solid than a clutch of hit singles. Lack of success and a paucity of newly released material may have made him an unfamiliar figure to younger audiences by the new millennium, but can hardly diminish the lustre of his output during the classic decades of the 1960s and 1970s. As a songwriter, musician, and craftsman in the studio he was exceptionally gifted. In the words of broadcaster Mark Radcliffe, he was the Midlands' answer to Ray Davies of the Kinks – 'an undervalued British pop genius', while according to Mat Snow of *Q Magazine* he was 'one of British pop music's greatest lost talents'. There are surely few who would disagree.

DISCOGRAPHY

Included below are month (if known) and year of release, label and UK catalogue number unless stated otherwise. Bootlegs are excluded, and for reasons of space only the most important reissues and compilations are listed. Several of The Move singles were reissued between 1979 and 1982 on the Cube, Old Gold and Cube/Dakota labels. All singles and albums are on vinyl up to 1990, and on CD thereafter unless otherwise stated. PS denotes picture sleeve for vinyl singles

SINGLES

GERRY LEVENE & THE AVENGERS

Dr Feelgood/Driving Me Wild (1.64) Decca F 11815

MIKE SHERIDAN & THE NIGHTRIDERS

Oh What A Sweet Thing That Was/Fabulous (4.64) Columbia DB 7302
Here I Stand/Lonely Weekends (1.65) Columbia DB 7462

MIKE SHERIDAN'S LOT

Take My Hand/Make Them Understand (8.65) Columbia DB 7677
Don't Turn Your Back On Me, Babe/Stop Look and Listen (12.65) Columbia DB 7798

DANNY KING'S MAYFAIR SET

Pretty Things/Youngblood (1.65) Columbia DB 7456

THE MOVE

Night of Fear/Disturbance (12.66) Deram DM 109
I Can Hear The Grass Grow/Wave The Flag And Stop The Train (3.67) Deram DM 117
Flowers in the Rain/(Here We Go Round The) Lemon Tree (9.67) Regal Zonophone RZ 3001
Fire Brigade/Walk Upon The Water (2.68) Regal Zonophone RZ 3005
Wild Tiger Woman/Omnibus (8.68) Regal Zonophone RZ 3012
Blackberry Way/Something (12.68) Regal Zonophone RZ 3015
Curly/This Time Tomorrow (7.69) Regal Zonophone RZ 3021
Brontosaurus/Lightning Never Strikes Twice (3.70) Regal Zonophone RZ 3026
When Alice Comes Back To The Farm/What? (10.70) Fly BUG 2
Ella James/No Time (5.71) Harvest HAR 5036 - withdrawn
Tonight/Don't Mess Me Up (5.71) Harvest HAR 5038
Chinatown/Down On The Bay (10.71) Harvest HAR 5043
Fire Brigade/ I Can Hear The Grass Grow/Night of Fear (4.72) Fly ECHO 104
California Man/Do Ya/Ella James (4.72) Harvest HAR 5050
Do Ya/No Time (9.74) Harvest HAR 5088
Flowers In The Rain/Move (8.07) Salvo SALVOSV002 – also limited fan-club only red vinyl
Flowers In The Rain/Beautiful Daughter/Feel Too Good (radio edit)/*Fire Brigade* (instrumental) (8.07) Salvo SALVOSCD002

ELECTRIC LIGHT ORCHESTRA

10538 Overture/1st Movement (Jumping Biz) (7.72) Harvest HAR 5053
Roll Over Beethoven/Queen Of The Hours (2.73) Harvest HAR 5063 (Roy Wood B-side only)

WIZZARD

Ball Park Incident/The Carlsberg Special (Pianos Demolished Phone 021 373 4472) (11.72) Harvest HAR 5062
See My Baby Jive/Bend Over Beethoven (3.73) Harvest HAR 5070
Angel Fingers (A Teen Ballad)/You Got The Jump On Me (7.73) Harvest HAR 5076
I Wish It Could Be Christmas Everyday/Rob Roy's Nightmare (A Bit More H.A.) (11.73) Warner Bros K16336, PS - withdrawn
I Wish It Could Be Christmas Everyday/Rob Roy's Nightmare (A Bit More H.A.) (11.73) Harvest HAR 5079, PS
Rock'n'Roll Winter (Looney's Tune)/Dream Of Unwin (4.74) Warner Bros K16357, PS
This Is The Story Of My Love (Baby)/ Nixture (8.74) Warner Bros K16434
Are You Ready To Rock/Marathon Man (12.74) Warner Bros K16336
Rattlesnake Roll/Can't Help My Feelings (10.75) Jet JET 758
Indiana Rainbow/The Thing Is This (This Is The Thing) (3.76) - credited to ROY WOOD'S WIZZARD on label
See My Baby Jive/Angel Fingers/ Ball Park Incident (3.76) Harvest HAR 5106
I Wish It Could Be Christmas Everyday/See My Baby Jive (11.78 and several subsequent years) Harvest HAR 5173, PS
I Wish It Could Be Christmas Everyday (extended party mix)/*See My Baby Jive/Forever* (11.84) Harvest HAR 5173, 12", PS

ROY WOOD

When Gran'ma Plays the Banjo/Wake Up (2.72) Harvest HAR 5048
Dear Elaine/Songs Of Praise (10.72) Harvest HAR 5057 - withdrawn
Dear Elaine/Songs Of Praise (7.73) Harvest HAR 5074
Forever/Music to Commit Suicide By (11.73) Harvest HAR 5078
Goin' Down The Road (A Scottish Reggae Song)/The Premium Bond Theme (5.74) Harvest HAR 5083
Oh What A Shame/Bengal Jig (5.75) Jet JET 754, PS
Look Thru' The Eyes of a Fool/Strider (11.75) Jet JET 761 – some copies pressed as *Looking Thru' The Eyes of a Fool*
Any Old Time Will Do/The Rain Came Down On Everything (8.76) Jet JET 785
Keep Your Hands On The Wheel/Giant Footsteps (11.78) Warner Bros K17248

(We're) On The Road Again/Saxmaniacs (5.79)   Automatic K17459, picture disc K17459P
Sing Out The Old/Watch This Space (12.80) Cheapskate CHEAP 12
Down to Zero/Olympic Flyer (4.81) EMI EMI 5203, PS
It's Not Easy/Moonriser (2.82) EMI EMI 5261, PS
O.T.T./Mystery Song (4.82) Woody/Speed SPEED 5
Under Fire/On Top of the World (5.85) Legacy LGY 24, PS
Under Fire (Mad Mix 1)/On Top of the World (5.85) Legacy LGYT 24, 12"
Sing Out The Old, Bring In The New/Sing Out The Old, Bring In The New (instrumental) (11.85) Legacy LGY 32, PS
Sing Out The Old, Bring In The New (extended version party mix)/Sing Out The Old, Bring In The New/Sing Out The Old, Bring In The New (instrumental) (11.85) Legacy LGYT 32, 12", PS
Raining In The City/Raining In The City (instrumental) (11.86) Legacy LGY 53, PS
1-2-3/Oh What A Shame (7.87) Jet JET 7048, PS
1-2-3 (extended version)/1-2-3/Oh What A Shame (7.87) Jet JET 13048, 12", PS

ROY WOOD AND ANNIE HASLAM

I Never Believed in Love/Inside my Life (10.77) Warner Bros K17028

ROY WOOD'S WIZZO BAND

The Stroll/Jubilee (6.77) Warner Bros K16961, PS
Dancin' At The Rainbow's End/Waiting At This Door (2.78) Warner Bros K17094

ROY WOOD'S HELICOPTERS

Rock City/Givin' Your Heart Away (11.80) Cheapskate CHEAP 6, PS
Green Glass Windows/The Driving Song (4.81) EMI EMI 5156, PS

THE ROCKERS

We Are The Boys (Who Make All The Noise)/Rockin' On The Stage (11.83) CBS A3929, PS
We Are The Boys (Who Make All The Noise), extended version/*Rockin' on the Stage* (11.83) CBS TA3929, 12", PS

DOCTOR AND THE MEDICS WITH ROY WOOD

Waterloo/Damaged Brains (10.86), IRS IRM 125, 12" IRMT 125, PS

ROY WOOD AND RICK WAKEMAN

Custer's Last Stand/Ocean City (11.88) President (Roy Wood A-side only)

ROY WOOD BIG BAND

I Wish It Could Be Christmas Everyday/Santa Claus is Coming to Town/I Wish It Could Be Christmas Everyday, soundcheck version/*Lion's Heart* (11.95) Woody 001CD

ROY WOOD AND THE WOMBLES
I Wish it Could Be a Wombling Merry Christmas Everyday (12.00) Dramatico DRAMCDS0001

EPs

THE MOVE

SOMETHING ELSE FROM THE MOVE: *So You Want To Be a Rock'n'Roll Star/Stephanie Knows Who/Something Else/It'll Be Me/Sunshine Help Me* (7.68) Regal Zonophone TRZ 2001 (33 rpm) PS

ALBUMS

Compilations are listed selectively

MIKE SHERIDAN AND THE NIGHTRIDERS

BIRMINGHAM BEAT: *No Other Guy/Tell Me What You're Gonna Do/Please Mr Postman/In Love/Brand New Cadillac/A Thing Of The Past/What A Sweet Thing That Was//Fabulous/Here I Stand/Lonely Weekends/Take My Hand/Make Them, Understand/Stop Look And Listen/Don't Turn Your Back On Me* (2.84) Edsel 120 (mono) – Roy does not appear on the first five tracks

THE MOVE

MOVE: *Yellow Rainbow/Kilroy was Here/(Here We Go Round The) Lemon Tree/Weekend/Walk Upon The Water/Flowers In The Rain/Hey Grandma//Useless Information/Zing Went The Strings Of My Heart/The Girl Outside/Fire Brigade/Mist On A Monday Morning/Cherry Blossom Clinic* (3.68) Regal Zonophone LRZ 1007 (mono), SLRZ 1007 (stereo)

SHAZAM: *Hello Susie/Beautiful Daughter/Cherry Blossom Clinic Revisited//Fields Of People/Don't Make My Baby Blue/The Last Thing On My Mind* (2.70) Regal Zonophone SLRZ 1012

LOOKING ON: *Looking On/Turkish Tram Conductor Blues/What?/When Alice Comes Back To The Farm//Open Up Said The World At The Door/Brontosaurus/Feel Too Good* (11.70) Fly FLY 1

MESSAGE FROM THE COUNTRY: *Message From the Country/Ella James/No Time/Don't Mess Me Up/Until Your Mama's Gone//It Wasn't My Idea To Dance/The Minister/Ben Crawley's Steel Company/Words Of Aaron/My Marge* (10.71) Harvest SHSP 4013

THE BBC SESSIONS: *You'd Better Believe Me/Night Of Fear/Stop Get A Hold Of Myself/Kilroy Was Here/Walk Upon The Water/I Can Hear The Grass Grow/Morning Dew/Flowers In The Rain/So You Want To Be a Rock'n'Roll Star/Stephanie Knows Who/Cherry Blossom Clinic/Hey*

Grandma/Fire Brigade/Weekend/ It'll Be Me/Useless Information/Kentucky Woman/Higher And Higher/Long Black Veil/Wild Tiger Woman/Piece Of My Heart/Blackberry Way/Goin' Back/California Girls/This Christian Life (1998) Strange Fruit SFRSCD069

MOVE: *Yellow Rainbow/Kilroy Was Here/(Here We Go Round The) Lemon Tree/Weekend/Walk Upon The Water/Flowers in the Rain/Hey Grandma//Useless Information/Zing Went The Strings Of My Heart/The Girl Outside/Fire Brigade/Mist on a Monday Morning/Cherry Blossom Clinic/Vote For Me/Disturbance/Night Of Fear/Wave The Flag And Stop The Train/I Can Hear The Grass Grow//Move Intro/Move/ Cherry Blossom Clinic/ Fire Brigade/Kilroy was Here/(Here We Go Round The) Lemon Tree/Weekend/Zing Went The Strings Of My Heart/Don't Throw Stones At Me/Mist on a Monday Morning/Vote For Me/Night Of Fear/The Girl Outside/Walk Upon The Water/Useless Information/Flowers In The Rain* (2007) Salvo SALVODCD207; CD1 mono, CD2 stereo

SHAZAM: *Hello Susie/Beautiful Daughter/Cherry Blossom Clinic Revisited//Fields of People/Don't Make My Baby Blue/The Last Thing On My Mind/This Time Tomorrow/A Certain Something/Curly/Wild Tiger Woman/Omnibus/That Certain Something/This Time Tomorrow/Blackberry Way* (2007) Salvo SALVOCD012

LOOKING ON: *Looking On/Turkish Tram Conductor Blues/What?/When Alice Comes Back To The Farm/Open Up Said The World At The Door/Brontosaurus/Feel Too Good/Lightnin' Never Strikes Twice/Looking On Part 1/Looking On Part 2/Turkish Tram Conductor Blues/ Open Up Said The World At The Door/Feel Too Good/The Duke Of Edinburgh's Lettuce* (2008) Salvo SALVOCD014

MESSAGE FROM THE COUNTRY: *Message From the Country/Ella James/No Time/Don't Mess Me Up/Until Your Mama's Gone//It Wasn't My Idea To Dance/The Minister/Ben Crawley's Steel Company/Words Of Aaron/My Marge/Tonight/Chinatown/Down On The Bay/Do Ya/California Man/Don't Mess Me Up/The Words Of Aaron/Do Ya* (2005) Harvest 09463 30342 2 8

THE MOVE ANTHOLOGY: *You're The One I Need/I Can't Hear You No More/Is It True/Respectable/Night of Fear/Disturbance/I Can Hear The Grass Grow (full-length version)/Move/Wave The Flag And Stop The Train/(Here We Go Round) The Lemon Tree/Flowers & Lemon Tea (Tony Visconti talks to the players...)/Flowers In The Rain/Cherry Blossom*

Clinic/Vote For Me/Fire Brigade (early piano version; rough mix)/Useless Information/Yellow Rainbow/Kilroy Was Here/Fire Brigade/The Girl Outside/Mist On A Monday Morning (enhanced stereo) /Flowers In The Rain (acoustic version; rough mix)/Simple Simon//Move Bolero (live)/It'll Be Me (live)/Too Much In Love (live)/Flowers In The Rain (live)/Fire Brigade (live)/Stephanie Knows Who (live)/Something Else (live)/So You Want To Be A Rock'n'Roll Star (live)/The Price Of Love (live)/Piece Of My Heart (live)/(Your Love Keeps Lifting Me) Higher And Higher (live)/Sunshine Help Me (live)//Somethin' Else (EP version)/Sunshine Help Me (EP version)/Wild Tiger Woman/Omnibus/Blackberry Way/A Certain Something/Curly/Second Class (She's Too Good For Me) (Part 1)/Second Class (She's Too Good For Me) (Part 2)/Beautiful Daughter/This Time Tomorrow/Hello Susie/Don't Make My Baby Blue/The Last Thing On My Mind/Open My Eyes (live at Fillmore West 1969)///I Can Hear The Grass Grow (Fillmore West 1969)/Brontosaurus (US promo edit)/When Alice Comes Back To The Farm/Turkish Tram Conductor Blues/Feel Too Good/Lightning Never Strikes Twice/Ella James/Tonight/Do Ya/Chinatown/California Man/The Duke Of Edinburgh's Lettuce (2008) Salvo SALVOBX406, 4-CD

LIVE AT THE FILLMORE 1969: *Open My Eyes/Don't Make My Baby Blue/Cherry Blossom Clinic Revisited/The Last Thing On My Mind/I Can Hear The Grass Grow/Fields Of People/Goin' Back/Hello Susie/Under The Ice/Introduction/Don't Make My Baby Blue/Cherry Blossom Clinic Revisited/The Last Thing On My Mind* (2011) Right Recordings, RIGHT16, 2-CD

LIVE AT THE FILLMORE 1969: *Open My Eyes/Don't Make My Baby Blue/Cherry Blossom Clinic Revisited/The Last Thing On My Mind/I Can Hear The Grass Grow/Fields Of People/Goin' Back/Hello Susie/Under The Ice* (2014) Right Recordings, BAD2LP205 – double LP, red vinyl

ELECTRIC LIGHT ORCHESTRA

ELECTRIC LIGHT ORCHESTRA: *10538 Overture/Look At Me Now/Nellie Takes Her Bow/Battle of Marston Moor (July 2nd 1644)//1st Movement (Jumping Biz)/Mr Radio/Manhattan Rumble (49th St Massacre)/Queen Of The Hours/Whisper in the Night* (11.71) Harvest SHVL 797; reissued 2001 as a double CD with additional tracks

E.L.O. 2 – Roy plays bass and cello, uncredited, on *In Old England Town (Boogie No. 2)/From The Sun To The World (Boogie No. 1)* (3.73) Harvest SHVL 806; reissued 2003 as a double CD with additional tracks

WIZZARD

WIZZARD BREW: *You Can Dance The Rock'n'Roll/Meet Me At The Jailhouse/Jolly Cup Of Tea//Buffalo Station-Get on Down to Memphis/Gotta Crush (About You)/Wear A Fast Gun* (3.73) Harvest SHSP 4025

INTRODUCING EDDY AND THE FALCONS: *Intro/Eddy's Rock/Brand New "88"/You Got Me Runnin'/I Dun Lotsa Cryin' Over You/This Is The Story Of My Love (Baby)//Everyday I Wonder/Crazy Jeans/Come Back Karen/We're Gonna Rock'n'Roll Tonight* (8.74) Warner Bros K56029

WIZZARD BREW: *You Can Dance The Rock'n'Roll/Meet Me At The Jailhouse/Jolly Cup Of Tea//Buffalo Station-Get on Down to Memphis/Gotta Crush (About You)/Wear A Fast Gun/Ball Park Incident/The Carlsberg Special/See My Baby Jive/Bend Over Beethoven/Angel Fingers/You Got The Jump On Me/Rob Roy's Nightmare/I Wish it Could be Christmas Everyday* (2006) Harvest 94637 12672

ROY WOOD & WIZZARD

MAIN STREET: *Main Street/Saxmaniax/The Fire In His Guitar/French Perfume/Take my Hand/Don't You Feel Better/Indiana Rainbow/I Should Have Known* (3.00) Edsel EDCD 626

ROY WOOD

BOULDERS: *Songs of Praise/Wake Up/Rock Down Low/Nancy Sing Me A Song/Dear Elaine//All The Way Over The Hill-The Irish Loafer (And His Hen)/Miss Clarke And The Computer/When Gran'ma Plays The Banjo/Rock Medley: Rockin' Shoes/She's Too Good For Me/Locomotive* (7.73) Harvest SHVL 803

MUSTARD: *Mustard/Any Old Time Will Do/The Rain Came Down On Everything/You Sure Got It Now//Why Does Such A Pretty Girl Sing Those Sad Songs/The Song/Look Thru The Eyes Of A Fool/Interlude/Get On Down Home* (11.75) Jet JETLP 12

ON THE ROAD AGAIN: *(We're) On the Road Again/Wings Over The Sea/Keep Your Hands On The Wheel/Colourful Lady/Road Rocket//Backtown Sinner/Jimmy Lad/Dancin' At The Rainbow's End/Another Night/Way Beyond The Rain* (1979) Warner Bros K56591

STARTING UP: *Red Cars Are After Me/Raining In The City/Under Fire/Turn Your Body To The Light//Starting Up/Keep It Steady/On Top Of The World/Ships In The Night* (1.87) Legacy LLP 106

BOULDERS: *Songs of Praise/Wake Up/Rock Down Low/Nancy Sing Me A Song/Dear Elaine//All The Way Over The Hill-The Irish Loafer (And His Hen)/Miss Clarke And The Computer/When Gran'ma Plays The Banjo/Rock Medley: Rockin' Shoes/She's Too Good For Me/Locomotive/Dear Elaine* (2007) Harvest CDSHVLR 803

ROY WOOD WIZZO BAND

SUPER ACTIVE WIZZO: *Life is Wonderful/Waitin' At This Door/Another Wrong Night//Sneakin'/Giant Footsteps (Jubilee)/Earthrise* (10.77) Warner Bros K56388

Selected compilations

In most cases, these include a mixture of tracks from one or more of the groups of which Roy Wood was formerly a member, as well as solo material

THE ROY WOOD STORY: *Make Them Understand/Night of Fear/I Can Hear the Grass Grow/Flowers in the Rain/Fire Brigade/Wild Tiger Woman/Blackberry Way//Curly/Brontosaurus/When Alice Comes Back to the Farm/Chinatown/Tonight/California Man//1st Movement (Jumping Biz)/Look At Me Now/Ball Park Incident/See My Baby Jive/Angel Fingers/I Wish It Could Be Christmas Everyday//When Gran'ma Plays The*

Banjo/Dear Elaine/Forever/Music To Commit Suicide By/Goin' Down The Road/The Premium Bond Theme (1976) Harvest SHDW 408, double – The first compilation to include all Move A-sides

THE SINGLES: *See My Baby Jive/Are You Ready To Rock/Oh What a Shame/Fire Brigade/Forever/I Can Hear the Grass Grow/O.T.T.//Blackberry Way/Angel Fingers/(We're) On The Road Again/Flowers in the Rain/Green Glass Windows/Keep Your Hands On The Wheel/Rock'n'Roll Winter/This Is The Story Of My Love (Baby)* (1982) Woody/Speed 1000 - The only Roy Wood compilation to chart. The second pressing also included *I Wish It Could Be Christmas Everyday*

EXOTIC MIXTURE, BEST OF SINGLES A's & B's: *When Gran'ma Plays The Banjo/Wake Up/Nancy Sing Me A Song/Dear Elaine/Songs Of Praise/Going Down The Road/The Premium Bond Theme/Forever/Music To Commit Suicide By/Oh What A Shame/Bengal Jig/Look Through The Eyes Of A Fool/Strider/Mustard/Indiana Rainbow/The Thing Is This/Any Old Time Will Do/The Rain Came Down On Everything/The Stroll/Saxmaniacs/Jubilee/I Never Believed In Love/Inside My Life/Dancing At The Rainbow's End/Waiting At The Door/(We're) On The Road Again/Rock City/Givin' Your Heart Away/Green Glass Windows/The Driving Song/It's Not Easy/Moonriser/We Are The Boys (Who Make All The Noise)/Rockin' On The Stage/Under Fire/On Top Of The World/Sing Out The Old-Bring In The New/Raining In The City/1-2-3* (2000) Repertoire REP 4744-WR, double

ROY WOOD: THE WIZZARD! GREATEST HITS AND MORE: *See My Baby Jive/Ball Park Incident/Angel Fingers (A Teen Ballad)/Forever/Olympic Flyer/Ella James/Dear Elaine/Moonriser/Green Glass Windows/Aerial Pictures/Airborne/The Premium Bond Theme/Goin' Down The Road (A Scottish Reggae Song)/The Driving Song/It's Not Easy/Down To Zero/Music To Commit Suicide By/Whisper In The Night/California Man/I Wish It Could Be Christmas Everyday/ Angel Fingers (A Teen Ballad) (Vocal Overdubs)* (2006) EMI 344 1362

LOOK THRU' THE EYES OF ROY WOOD: *Intro/Eddy's Rock/Are You Ready To Rock/Rock 'N' Roll Winter (Loony's Tune)/Everyday I Wonder/We're Gonna Rock 'N' Roll Tonight/Looking Thru' The Eyes Of A Fool/Any Old Time Will Do/Why Does Such A Pretty Girl Sing Those Sad Songs/Bengal Jig/Kenny Everett Jingle/The Song/Ball Park Incident* (live)*/Angel Fingers (A Teen Ballad)* (live)*/Forever* (live)*/This Is The Story Of My Love (Baby)* (live)*//Rattlesnake Roll/Oh What A Shame/The Rain*

Came Down On Everything/Indiana Rainbow/Human Cannonball/Main Street/The Thing Is This (This Is The Thing)/Starting Up/Hot Cars/Raining In The City/Red Cars Are After Me/1-2-3/Under Fire/Sing Out The Old, Bring In The New (2007) Sanctuary CMQSS1300, double

MUSIC BOOK: *California Man* (live)*/Ball Park Incident/Forever/Oh What A Shame/Fire Brigade/French Perfume/Down To Zero/Raining In The City/I Can Hear The Grass Grow* [Status Quo]*/Beautiful Daughter/Tonight/Lion's Heart/Look Thru' The Eyes Of A Fool/Dear Elaine/Main Street/New York City/Givin' Your Heart Away/Sing Out The Old...Bring In The New/See My Baby Jive/Starting Up/Any Old Time Will Do/Miss Clark And The Computer/Green Glass Windows/R. U. Red E 2 Rock/Chinatown/Flowers In The Rain* [Nancy Sinatra]*/ Why Does Such A Pretty Girl (Sing Those Sad Songs)/Brontosaurus/Olympic Flyer/Angel Fingers/Keep Your Hands On The Wheel/Aerial Pictures/This Is The Story Of My Love (Baby)/Blackberry Way/I Wish It Could Be Christmas Everyday/First Movement* (2011) Harvest 099973 122128, double

ORIGINAL ALBUM SERIES: 5 CDs comprising 'Message From The Country'; 'Electric Light Orchestra'; 'Boulders'; 'Wizzard Brew'; 'On The Road Again', Parlophone/Warner Bros 2564621329 (2014), as per original LP releases without bonus tracks

Cameo appearances

ALL THIS AND WORLD WAR II, Original Motion Picture Soundtrack (RIVA RIVLP 2 [double], 1976). Roy Wood sings *Lovely Rita* and *Polythene Pam*, with London Symphony Orchestra and Royal Philharmonic Orchestra

HEROES AND VILLAINS, The Concert to Celebrate 15 Years of Radio 1, recorded live at the Odeon, Hammersmith, 21 September 1982 (Dakota OTA 1001, 1982). Carl Wayne sings *Flowers in the Rain*, with Magnum

ARRESTED – THE MUSIC OF THE POLICE, Royal Philharmonic Orchestra and Friends (RCA RCALP 8001, 1983). Roy Wood sings *Message in a Bottle* with Gary Moore (guitar), Neil Murray (bass), Ian Paice (drums)

Cover versions of Roy Wood songs on singles

Many of these were also produced by Roy Wood and feature him on instruments and/or backing vocals

BLUES MAGOOS - *I Can Hear The Grass Grow* (Mercury 72838, 1967, USA only)
IDLE RACE - *(Here We Go Round) The Lemon Tree* (Liberty 55097, 1967, USA only)
FORTUNES - *Fire Brigade* (United Artists UA 500280, 1968, USA, Holland UK)
CLIFF BENNETT & HIS BAND- *You're Breaking Me Up* (Parlophone R5691, 1968)
LEATHER SANDWICH – *Kilroy Was Here* (Philips BF 414, 1968, Australia)
AMEN CORNER - *Hello Susie* (Immediate IM 081, 1969) - the only one to chart in the UK
CASUALS - *Caroline* (Decca F22969, 1969)
ACID GALLERY - *Dance Round The Maypole* (CBS 4608, 1969)
MAIL - *Omnibus* (Parlophone R5916, 1971)
NANCY SINATRA - *Flowers In the Rain* (Reprise K14138, 1971)
NASHVILLE TEENS - *Ella James* (Parlophone R5925, 1972)
GRAHAM BONNET – *Whisper In The Night* (RCA RCA 2230, 1972)
JOHN PERRY - *Nancy Sing Me A Song* (Philips, 1973)
AYSHEA - *Farewell* (Harvest HAR 5073, 1973)
NEIL REID - *Hazel Eyes* (Philips 6006 389, 1974)
SMILEY & CO - *You Got Me Runnin'* (Jet JET 759, 1975)
FLASH CADILLAC & THE CONTINENTAL KIDS - *See My Baby Jive* (Private Stock PVT 92, 1977)
CHEAP TRICK - *California Man* (Epic EPC 6427, 1978)
TIM CURRY - *Brontosaurus* (A&M 57383, 1978), B-side of *I Will*
GARY HOLTON & CASINO STEEL – *Blackberry Way* (Polydor 2052 209, 1982)
CHARLIE [CARL] WAYNE - *Aerial Pictures/Colourful Lady* (Jet JET 7022, 1982)
JIM DAVIDSON - *California Man* (CBS RELAX 3, 1984), B-side of *Silver Among The Gold*, produced by Jim Davidson and Rick Price
BUDDY CURTESS & THE GRASSHOPPERS – *Hello Susie* (Mercury MERCURY 2, 1986)

Roy Wood guest appearances and productions

JIMI HENDRIX EXPERIENCE – 'Axis Bold As Love' (Track 613 003, 1967), Roy and other members of the Move sing backing vocals on *You Got Me Floatin'*
BEGGARS OPERA - *Two Timing Woman* (Vertigo 6059 088, 1973), brass arrangement by Roy
BEV BEVAN - *Heavyhead* (Jet JET 777, 1976), B-side of *Let There be Drums*, Roy plays saxophone
RENAISSANCE – 'Song For All Seasons' (Warner Bros K56450, 1977), uncredited appearance by Roy
ANNIE HASLAM – 'Annie In Wonderland' Warner Bros K56453, 1977)
LOUIS CLARK – '(per-spek-tiv)n' (Jet JETLP 218, 1979), Roy plays guitar and sitar
DARTS - *Dart Attack* (Magnet MAGL 5030, 1979), Roy plays several instruments, sings backing vocals (uncredited), and also produces. 2011 remastered reissue includes *Sing Out The Old...Bring In The New* (AIS 6534003, 2011)
PARANOIDS - *Love Job* (Hurricane FIRE 14, 1980)
P45 – *Right Direction* (Jet, JET 190, 1980)
LOUIS CLARK - *Hooked on Christmas*, including *I Wish It Could Be Christmas Everyday* (Jet JET 7031, 1982)
ROYAL PHILHARMONIC ORCHESTRA – 'The Royal Philharmonic Orchestra Plays The Beatles' (Evolution SRFL 1001, 1982), Roy sings *Happy Christmas War Is Over*, and plays bagpipes on *Mull of Kintyre*
ROYAL PHILHARMONIC ORCHESTRA – 'Hooked On Classics 3' (K-Tel ONE 1226, 1983), Roy plays bagpipes on *Scotland the Brave*
CRUELLA DE VILLE - *Hong Kong Swing/Drunken Uncle John* (Parlophone R6075, 1984), co-produced by Roy, Dick Plant and the group
CRUELLA DE VILLE - *Oceans* (CPL CPL-5, 1984), one of three tracks on a maxi-single, A-side *I'll Do the Talking*
ALAN RANDALL - *Eeh Bah Gum, Give It Some Clog* (Legacy LGY 27, 12" LGYT 27, 1985)
TEMPEST - *Hell Fire* (Mack MAK 001, 1985)

Bootlegs

Bootlegs are illegal, and the writers and performers of material used on these receive no remuneration from their sales. The author is aware of the existence of various Roy Wood bootleg albums and CDs, spanning all stages of his career and of widely varying quality, mostly in-concert tapes but some also including elusive material originally released on poorly-selling and now ultra-collectable singles. These can generally be tracked down and sought out by those who are determined enough.

BIBLIOGRAPHY

Arden, Don, and Wall, Mick, *Mr Big: Ozzy, Sharon and My Life as the Godfather of Rock* (Robson, 2004)
Bevan, Bev, *The Electric Light Orchestra Story* (Mushroom, 1980)
Caiger, Rob, Electric Light Orchestra (in 'Record Collector', October 1994)
Clayson, Alan, Ace Kefford (interview) (in 'Record Collector', July 1994)
Devine, Campbell, *All The Young Dudes: Mott The Hoople and Ian Hunter, the Official Biography* (Cherry Red, 1998)
Frame, Pete, *The Complete Rock Family Trees* (Omnibus, 1983)
Hardy, Phil, The Move is dead, long live Wizzard and ELO (in 'Let It Rock', January 1973)
Harvey, Peter, The Great Ones: Roy Wood (in 'Record Mirror', 4 May 1974)
Hogg, Brian, The Move (in 'Record Collector', March 1981)
Paytress, Mark, The Move (in 'Record Collector', July 1994); Watching the grass grow: The Move's Birmingham roots (in 'Record Collector', August 1994)
Sharp, Ken, Roy Wood (interview) (in 'Record Collector', July and August 1994)
Thompson, Dave, *Sparks: No. 1 Songs In Heaven* (Cherry Red, 2009)
Tobler, John, and Grundy, Stuart, *The Record Producers* (BBC, 1982)
Van der Kiste, John, Roy Wood & Wizzard (in 'Record Collector', April 1986)
Visconti, Tony, *Bowie, Bolan and The Brooklyn Boy* (HarperCollins, 2007)
Wanda, Jürgen, *Blackberry Way: Move, Electric Light Orchestra, Roy Wood, Jeff Lynne und Steve Gibbons Band* (Star Cluster, 1996) – in German
Weiner, Andrew, Lookin' Back: The Move (in 'New Musical Express', 30 March 1974)

Disc And Music Echo
Face The Music
Keep On Rockin'
Melody Maker
New Musical Express
Record Mirror
Royzone
Sounds
Trouser Press
Useless Information (The Move/Roy Wood online mailing list)

Miscellaneous press and music press cuttings from various collections, mostly undated; miscellaneous online interviews, with particular thanks to the following websites

Roy Wood official website
http://www.roywood.co.uk/

Cherry Blossom Clinic
http://www.cherryblossomclinic.freeserve.co.uk/

Face the Music online
http://www.ftmusic.com/

Useless Information, Move mailing list
http://www.eskimo.com/~noanswer/move_archives/movearchives.html

45cat
http://www.45cat.com/

The author

John Van der Kiste is the author, with Derek Wadeson, of *Beyond The Summertime: The Mungo Jerry Story*. He has reviewed records and books for various national, local and independent publications and websites, was commissioned to contribute the entries on Brian Connolly and Lena Zavaroni to the *Oxford Dictionary of National Biography*, various entries to *Guinness Rockopaedia*, and the booklet notes to CDs by The Move, Wizzard, Roy Wood and other acts. He has also written and published several historical and royal biographies, works of local history and true crime, plays and fiction. He lives in Devon.

For a complete list of titles available, please visit Amazon.co.uk/Amazon.com

Printed in Great Britain
by Amazon.co.uk, Ltd.,
Marston Gate.